Difficult

Beginnings

Three Works on the Bodhisattva Path

CANDRAGOMIN

Translated, with commentary by Mark Tatz

SHAMBHALA · Boston & London · 1985

Shambhala Publications, Inc.
Horticultural Hall
300 Massachusetts Avenue
Boston, Massachusetts 02115
www.shambhala.com

Printed in the United States of America

Distributed in the United States by Random House, Inc.,
and in Canada by Random House of Canada Ltd

LIBRARY OF CONGRESS CATALOGING-IN-PUBLICATION DATA

Candragomin.
Difficult beginnings.
1. Religious life (Mahayana Buddhism) 2. Bodhisattva (The concept)
ISBN 1-57062-670-7
ISBN 0-394-54530 (Random House)
BQ7440.C362513 1983 83-2317
294.3′444
BVG 01

*Frontispiece/*Candragomin and the major events in his life, according to Tibetan historical tradition; a *thang-ka* by the late Topgyal of Tashijong.

To Hsüan Tsang

Contents

Introduction

Bodhisattva Theory and Practice

The Mahāyāna, as it emerges in India, infuses new life in old forms. Its predecessors, in the centuries after the time of the Buddha (sixth–fifth centuries B.C.), developed unique methods for understanding the nature of reality and for achieving liberation from the cycle of birth and death. The Mahāyāna, calling itself the Greater Vehicle, begins by the first century B.C. to coalesce around elements of the existing schools that are dissatisfied with the state of philosophy and practice.

In philosophy, the older schools have grown detailed to the point of pettiness in the enumeration, classification and analysis of phenomena—the "dharma theory" of Abhidharma works. The Mahāyāna makes emptiness (śūnyatā) the basis of a more profound system for the examination of reality. The concept of emptiness, however, is not new. In even the earliest Buddhist systems the key to liberation is to understand the doctrine of selflessness (anātman), which was formulated by the Buddha to refute what Kalupahana terms "an essentialist epistemology and metaphysic."[1]

The self (ātman), which is proposed in the Upaniṣads as a transcendent reality, is regarded by Buddhists as nothing more than an empty concept, with no more substance than a "rabbit's horn." Buddhists analyze the human individual into five aggregates (skandha) of phenomena: material elements (rūpa), feelings (vedanā), notions (saṁjñā), karmic formations (saṁskāra) and consciousness (vijñāna). No one of these, nor their totality can be connected, as the brahmanical schools would have it, with an abstract, timeless substrate of existence such as "self" or "soul." So the set of aggregates is characterized as "empty of self." The intention is not to deny personality in a working sense, the empirical "self." It is meant rather to refute the postulation of an absolute. In place of the static, unified ātman-brahman picture of the Upaniṣads, Buddhism presents the image of a pluralistic flow of phenomena or *dharmas* through time and space. The external world and the human personality are not to be considered as identical in nature to any single principle, for they are in continual flux; they represent the interaction of discrete, diverse elements which are impermanent.

Theoreticians of the Mahāyāna extend the notion of emptiness to all phenomena. Oneself and the world are collections of dharmas with no abiding essence. These dharmas themselves, furthermore, exist only in interdependence. Being impermanent and thus dependent, they themselves have no individual essence. For example, the mark of fire is heat. This might be said to constitute its essence. But fire requires for its arising the presence of various causes and conditions: air, fuel, combustion. Fire does not exist independently and cannot be said to really exist. So we have in the Mahāyāna, "emptiness of phenomena": emptiness of an abiding principle in any entity.

This expansion upon Buddhist principles is made in such early Mahāyāna scriptures (sūtra) as the Perfection of Wisdom (prajñāpāramitā). Just as prominent in these scriptures is the bodhisattva ideal. Like the deepening of existing philosophy, the broadening of practice is not based upon any concept previously unknown. Rather, it is the emphasis which mahāyānists place upon "bodhisattva" that distinguishes them from other schools. The bodhisattva may be characterized as a "future buddha." His/her goal is buddhahood, "awakening." The bodhisattva ideal appears quite clearly in the earlier scriptures. The historical Buddha is an example of its achievement. His past lives as a bodhisattva are documented in legendary form as the collection of Jātaka tales. How does this differ from the goal of other schools? Tradition classifies the paths to liberation as three: arhatship, independent (pratyeka) buddhahood and the full, complete and perfect awakening of a buddha. The arhat is said to succeed, under the tutelage of a teacher, in eliminating karma and its residues, thus freeing himself from rebirth. The independent buddha accomplishes the same feat without the aid of a teacher, for he lives his last life, at least, in an age in which no buddha appears. The bodhisattva eliminates karma as well, but he is in no rush to escape from birth and death. Instead, he develops a set of qualities that enable him to teach and guide others. The miraculous powers and capabilities developed by the bodhisattva are documented in Har Dayal's *The Boḍhisattva Doctrine.*[2] His is a longer path, with a more vast and detailed set of practices.

Only one of the pre-Mahāyāna schools has survived to modern times, though tradition counts them as eighteen. The Sthaviravāda (Pali: Theravāda) concentrates its attention upon the arhat ideal as being the more readily attainable. This would appear to be typical for many of those schools that disappeared. The bodhisattva ideal is known to them, but reserved to individuals of special capacity.

The tone of many early Mahāyāna scriptures compels one to admit that there is, from the beginning, antipathy toward the earlier schools. Those that espouse only the arhat ideal are judged as inferior. Hence the term Lesser Vehicle (Hīnayāna) applied to them, or the slightly less disparaging Vehicle of the Auditors (Śrāvakayāna). Just as mahāyānists attempt to lay aside scholastic nitpicking and to broaden their philosophic vistas, what is perceived as a narrow and stultifying monastic ethic is transformed in light of the aim of saving the whole world. The Mahāyāna is "greater" in that it enfolds the entire universe of creatures within its religious aims. So in early Mahāyāna the bodhisattva figure arises, enlarged and cosmic, above that of the arhat-disciple. His is the starring role in such early scriptures as the *Perfection of Wisdom* in its various recensions, the *Skill in Means* (upāya-kauśalya), the *Kāśyapa Chapter* of the Ratnakūṭa collection, and the *Samādhirāja.*

In terms of practice then, the Mahāyāna does not divorce itself from the schools that precede it. At times in the scriptures themselves, and more especially in the works of scholars who in their treatises (śāstra) mold the new ideal into a system, new terms and institutions are patterned upon existing models. The fulcrum of the bodhisattva's career is his vow (saṁvara) to bring himself and all others to awakening. Discussion of the vow is patterned upon what Asaṅga refers to as *prātimokṣa,* or lay and monastic vows.

Prātimokṣa refers originally to the fortnightly recitation of rules by monks and their ceremonial confession of failings.[3] Its application is extended to the monastic rule of nuns when the *Bhikṣuṇī-prātimokṣa* is formulated later. By Asaṅga it is made to refer to both lay and monastic codes—the corpus of Lesser Vehicle ethics. In Buddhist usage of the term, "vow" prescribes an ethic or moral code (śīla) that is composed of detailed trainings (śikṣā). The laity have five trainings: their precepts against killing, stealing, adultery, lying and taking intoxicants. Precepts for monks and nuns number 258 and 371 respectively.[4] Monastic trainings incorporate not only the natural (prākṛta) law that the monastic hold in common with the laity—not killing and so forth—but also special artificial or prescriptive (pratikṣepaṇa) legislation formulated in the monastic discipline (vinaya) to establish a lifestyle suited to preservation of the teachings and the rapid attainment of liberation. Celibacy, poverty, group living and so forth are not a natural morality in the sense that not killing or stealing are. But by them the monk or nun establishes the basis of renunciation, which is a necessary circumstance for making rapid progress on the path.

Bodhisattva trainings, by contrast, stem from the vow to bring all beings to liberation. The bodhisattva is therefore permitted much that is forbidden the monastic—anything, in fact, that has at heart the welfare of others. For the bodhisattva who is also a monastic, this may include the accumulation of wealth and even, in an extremity, uncelibacy. His vow may also, when the occasion warrants, supersede the natural morality of the layperson.

Nevertheless, the bodhisattva vow is clearly based upon prātimokṣa. In the "Chapter on Ethics" (Chapter Ten) of the *Bodhisattva-bhūmi,* Asaṅga specifies that an aspirant to the bodhisattva vow is either lay or monastic and this is generally taken to indicate that he or she *must* already be holding the prātimokṣa vow in its lay or monastic form (Skt.Dutt 105.8).

In its presentation by Asaṅga, the ceremony for taking the bodhisattva vow parallels the ceremony for taking on the prātimokṣa. Details of the ceremony also resemble those of prātimokṣa, as do details of the system of contradictions to the vow. Much of the content of bodhisattva vow literature is new, but the forms are familiar to all Buddhists. (Such is not the case with the still later sets of "pledges" [samaya] belonging to the Vajrayāna, also referred to upon occasion as a "vow.") Some of the similarities and contrasts will be indicated in the notes to the *Twenty Verses* below.

The rules of prātimokṣa deal for the most part with physical or mental actions, for they regulate the lay and monastic styles of life. The monk may not take food in the afternoon, for example, nor may he sit in private with a woman. In the bodhisattva ethic, thought and attitude are of primary importance, for the bodhisattva is distinguished from ordinary monk and layman by his goal and his attitude. A number of bodhisattva rules deal expressly with mental action—in fact, intention is a crucial element in all possible infractions of the bodhisattva vow. A proper attitude or intention (āśaya) is therefore prerequisite for taking this vow. One must have developed the aspiration, also translated "resolve" (praṇidhāna) to attain buddhahood. The generation (cittotpāda) of this aspiration is discussed in a previous chapter (no. 2) of the *Bodhisattva-bhūmi.*

Aspiration and vow-taking become topics of Buddhist literary endeavor. The ceremony for taking the vow, and the commitments entailed by it, undergo technical refinement and exegesis over the centuries. Generation of the aspiration, originally presented by scriptures in ceremonial form as well (for example, the Bhadracari resolve of the *Gaṇḍavyūha-sūtra),* becomes a more subjective genre, merging into *kāvya,* high poetry.[5]

So also does confession (deśana, nt.) come to be expressed in kāvya form. Confession is the antidote prescribed for most failings in keeping the bodhisattva vow, as it is to most monastic misdeeds. One ideally makes confession to superiors or to colleagues, but this is not essential for the bodhisattva. The function of confession is to generate regret for the misdeed or failing and to prevent its recurrence in the future; this can be accomplished by confession "within one's own mind" (*Twenty Verses* 8d). So Candragomin's *Confession* is a musing and a contemplation upon his failings along the path.

These three genres can be treated as a set. After making the aspiration, one embarks upon the bodhisattva course by taking the vow. Thereafter, one is held on course by periodic reexamination and self-criticism in the form of confession, analyzing one's practice in terms of the vowed commitments.

Candragomin

Candragomin, the seventh-century philosopher-poet who dwelt at the Buddhist university of Nālandā for some years, composed works in all three genres that survive in Tibetan translation.[6] For these and other works, and for the accounts of his life, Candragomin is regarded, in the Indo-Tibetan tradition, as an exemplar of the bodhisattva ideal. The Tibetan historian Tāranātha classes Candragomin with Śāntideva as the "two wonderful master-teachers (ācārya)" of Indian Buddhism.[7] The latter, an exponent of Mādhyamika philosophy, is the better known because his major works, the *Bodhicaryāvatāra* and the *Śikṣāsamuccaya,* survive in their original Sanskrit form as well as in Tibetan translation. Candragomin taught the bodhisattva path from Yogācāra sources. In his time, before the great doctrinal syntheses that attempted to smooth the conflicts and inconsistencies within the Buddhist fold, there was lively debate not only at doctrinal points at issue between the Buddhist schools, but on practical issues as well. Tāranātha, a historian with searching intellect and a sense of the dramatic, makes some of this evident in his account of Candragomin.

Candragomin's salient characteristic for the historian is his versatility. He is a layman (upāsaka). The name Candragomin indicates his lay status, *gomin* (Tib. btsun-pa) being the title of high respect for a lay adherent, the equivalent of *bhadanta* for a monk. He corresponds to our conception of a renaissance man, being an embodiment of the classical Indian ideal of a cultured cosmopolitan (nāgaraka) who is knowledgeable in the arts, science and literature of the day. Candragomin and King Harṣa, who preceded him by half a century, are credited with the only two dramas (nāṭaka) that are to be found in the Tengyur (bstan-'gyur) collection of the Tibetan sacred canon (Jātaka section). The Chinese pilgrim I Tsing relates that Candragomin's was sung and danced by all the peoples of eastern India.[8]

For the historian, Candragomin's life is a paradigm of teaching and giving in innumerable ways, as much a fulfillment of the bodhisattva ideal as can be achieved on the level of ordinary human existence. Nor, according to some thinkers of Candragomin's time, could this role be lived by the śramaṇa or ascetic, or by anyone who must hold to monastic vows. For to live up to the bodhisattva vow of helping all people in all ways requires at the outset broadmindedness, liberality and adaptability and, in the process, incursions into fields forbidden the monastic.

So says Śāntarakṣita in his comment to Candragomin's *Twenty Verses.* In discussing the line (11b) "Doing little for the welfare of living beings" (as a fault in regard to the bodhisattva vow), he says, "by maintaining both vows, one should be understood to have relinquished the welfare of others, and to be intent on one's own."[9] And in the context of the next line ("With mercy there is no [deed] without virtue") he describes circumstances in which precepts of natural morality may be violated. For example:

Accordingly, the bodhisattva, for sentient beings inclined to dance, song and instrumental music, and for those inclined to tales of kings and robbers, food and drink, prostitutes and street scenes, is learned in the varieties of dance, song, music and narrative. With a merciful intention he pleases them with varieties of narrative containing dance, song and music and endowed with idle chatter. He bends them to submission to his will and influence. Having drawn them in to listen to his words, he moves them from an unwholesome to a wholesome situation.

So, although there is idle chatter (sambhinna-pralāpa) on the part of the bodhisattva, no fault ensues, but rather a spread of much merit.[10]

Candragomin's "four hundred and thirty-two" works include writings on logic, poetry, drama, grammar, astrology, medicine (by the practice of which he is said by Tāranātha to have cured Siṁhala Island of a plague of leprosy; cf. *Confession*, verse 41 below) and philosophy. In fact, the celestial bodhisattva Tārā intercedes at one point to turn his attention back toward sacred subjects (cf. ibid., v. 8 on ending his reliance upon "the commonplace"). He contributes to the development of tantric ritual with numerous works on Avalokiteśvara, Tārā and other deities. Among his theoretical writings, those on the bodhisattva path have greatest fame.

As is common in the histories, Candragomin is made to embody one side of a religious conflict. He upholds the Buddhist literary tradition, as heir to Aśvaghoṣa and others, against his brahmanical counterparts. Especially, he places Buddhist linguistic science on a par with theirs. Although there is nothing doctrinal in his presentation of grammar, his work shows that the science can be investigated without presupposing the divinity of sound and without dealing with the Vedas.

On the Buddhist front, much space is devoted to Candragomin's seven-year rivalry with Candrakīrti at Nālandā. Gomin upholds the Cittamātra or Mind-only, Kīrti the Mādhyamika. Little of the content of the debate is related,[11] although it is stated that the contest generates so much interest that even the village children set themselves as judges, singing the verse:

O the works of the noble Nāgārjuna,
To some are medicine, to some poisonous;
The works of Ajita and noble Asaṅga,
Are a very nectar for all the people.[12]

The Mādhyamika, as the children imply, outlines a conception of emptiness so subtle that it can easily be misinterpreted with disastrous consequence. Nāgārjuna himself has admitted as much (*Kārikās* 24.11-12, etc.). The Yogācāra system of Maitreya (titled Ajita, "the Unvanquished") and Asaṅga is the truly Greater Vehicle in that it leads persons of all aptitudes and capacities gradually to awakening.

The historian has a special interest in the human side of the confrontation, and in Candragomin as an individual who lives the bodhisattva ethic and who is able to incorporate tantric accomplishment (siddhi) into his daily life.

The debate originates, according to Tāranātha, from Candragomin's mode of arrival and the offense it gives to Kīrti. The latter is defending the doctrine against all comers, as is the practice of the day, outside the walls of Nālandā. Upon being challenged by him, "What subjects do you know?" Candragomin mentions three works that indicate to his interrogator that he is the famous scholar of that name. Kīrti suggests that he be welcomed into the university by the entire monastic community. Gomin demurs, objecting that he is but a layman. Kīrti arranges for three chariots to enter side by side, the middle one bearing a statue of Mañjuśrī, the others bearing the two Candras. In this way, the community will appear to be welcoming Mañjuśrī. As the procession approaches the university gates, Candragomin composes a praise of the divinity.[13] The image turns its head to listen. In the ensuing uproar, Gomin's chariot pulls ahead. Kīrti takes this as a slight and determines to debate him. The debate only comes to an end when Kīrti discovers his opponent being tutored by a stone image of Avalokiteśvara, and accuses the celestial bodhisattva of partiality.

In the course of their rivalry, Gomin is made to appear a warmhearted bodhisattva, Kīrti a proud monk. On one occasion a poor old woman, seeking dowry with which to marry her daughter, hears of Kīrti's great wealth and approaches him for a gift. He admits to possessing a little money, but says that he is keeping it for the temple and the monastic community, and sends her over to Gomin. Candragomin owns nothing but the robes upon his body and a copy of the *Perfection of Wisdom* scripture. But his sympathy for her brings tears to his eyes. He paints a portrait of Tārā on the wall and composes a praise of her.[14] The image removes her precious ornaments as a gift.

In another incident Candragomin discovers that his rival's work on grammar is superior to his own. So he tosses his own in a well. The bodhisattva Tārā appears and advises him to recover it. His own work is fit to survive, she says, and not that of Candrakīrti, because the latter composed his grammar out of conceit for his erudition, and Candragomin out of concern for the welfare of others.

The historian is selecting his materials in order to make a

moral judgment. But it should be borne in mind that the histories, beginning with that of Bu-ston (pron. Pu-tön), are intended to function as adjuncts to the sacred canon, and to illustrate its development and contents. Hence the picture drawn by Tāranātha of Candragomin is based in large part upon those of his works that survive in it.

Candragomin's works were composed in classical Sanskrit. Only those among them that expound the Cāndra system of grammar, the attribution of which is doubtful, and the *Letter to a Friend* (śiṣya-lekha) survive in the original. The latter is didactic kāvya, like the *Confession.* The three translated here are only preserved in Tibetan translation. This circumstance is more unfortunate than it would be in the case of a mere philosopher such as Candrakīrti, for Candragomin is known to Indian tradition as a poet. This makes for difficulties of translation into Tibetan and of retranslation into English as well. The full import of the original is impossible to determine even in the Tibetan. As with all translation of poetry, however, an honest attempt to render the style and the meaning can be made. In discussing these three, the poetic value will not be disregarded.

Aspiration

Candragomin's Resolve (candragomi-praṇidhāna) consists of eleven verses, probably in śloka form, surviving in a Tibetan translation into seven-syllable pada. An extra line is found between verses eight and nine, apparently a peculiarity of the translation. Alliterative and other poetic techniques are not easily discernible from the Tibetan, but one can surmise that a number of lines could be read, in the original, in more than one way—a type of ambiguity and word-play common in Buddhist kāvya.[15] Technical terms are the stuff of the poem, beginning with karma and ending with buddhahood. The author resolves upon a good series of rebirths in contact with the Dharma, the pursuance of scholarship, practice, cultivation of virtue and of the arts and, in general, fulfillment of the ten bodhisattva perfections for the sake of others. According to the colophon, the translation was done by the monk (bhikṣu) Nyi-ma rgyal-mtshan dpal-bzang-po (pron. Nyi-ma gyal-tsen pä-sang-po, thirteenth–fourteenth centuries) in the city of Kaṭhmandu (yam-bu'i grong-khyer) in consultation with the Nepalese paṇḍita Jetakarṇa.

Vow

The *Twenty Verses on the Bodhisattva Vow* (bodhisattva-saṁvara-viṁśaka) is a mnemonic condensation of the "Chapter on Ethics" of the *Bodhisattva-bhūmi.* Only verse four of Candragomin's work promulgates an idea not found in his source. In Tibet it has been used as a study aid and as a basis for exposition of the bodhisattva vow. Presumably, it was used thus in India as well. The translation into Tibetan dates from the Early Spread of Buddhism into Tibet (ninth–tenth centuries), when it was done in conjunction with the commentary to it by Śāntarakṣita, which follows it in the sacred canon (0 no. 5583). The translator is given in the colophon (to the commentary) as Mañjuśrīvarman, in consultation with the Indian preceptor (upādhyāya) Vidyākarasiṁha. In syntax and terminology the translation of the commentary is nearly identical to that of the "Chapter on Ethics."

The translation of the *Twenty Verses* and its commentary that comes down to us is more than likely a retranslation done near the end of the Early Spread after translation of the *Bodhisattva-bhūmi* had been completed by others. According to Bu-ston, earlier translations of texts by Śāntarakṣita and others had to be redone, by a group including Mañjuśrīvarman, to establish terminological and grammatical consistency.[16] The *Twenty Verses* and its commentary would have been, in this view, among the first—if not the very first—translations done by Śāntarakṣita himself. He is known for having emphasized the bodhisattva path, being referred to by the Tibetans as "the preceptor bodhisattva." His first recorded act in Tibet was to ceremonially transmit the vow to Gsal-snang (pron. Sä-nang), governor of Mang-yul near the border with Nepal, who assumed the bodhisattva name Ye-shes dbang-po (pron. Ye-shay wang-po, Skt. Jñānendra).[17] Although the assumption of an initiation name is characteristic of transmission of the bodhisattva vow, this ceremony may in fact have been only the *cittotpāda*, generation of the aspiration, for there is no indication that Gsal-snang held any prātimokṣa vow at the time. Śāntarakṣita is also held responsible for transmission of prātimokṣa, but this occurred during his second visit to Tibet, when he gave lay ordination and then monastic ordination to the first seven "men of trial" (including Gsal-snang) at the monastery of Bsam-yas (pron. Sam-yä).[18] The verses and commentary must have been translated as part of the training of these monks. One might further surmise that the commentary was in fact composed in Tibet by Śāntarakṣita for this purpose, on the model of existing Indian commentaries, for in substance and in wording it scarcely differs from corresponding passages of the "Chapter on Ethics." Additions made by him seem to address monks not yet overly familiar with the monastic discipline.[19]

The *Twenty Verses* appears in other formats dating from this early period of Buddhism in Tibet. Especially significant is the role it played in the Sino-Tibetan school of Tun Huang, which flourished under the tutelage of the Chinese monk-translator Fa Ch'eng during the Tibetan occupation of that area in the ninth and tenth centuries. Wou Fa Ch'eng, who translated the *Twenty Verses* from Tibetan into Chinese, has been identified by Ueyama as the translator 'Gos/Wou Chos-grub (pron. Gö Chö-drub, Skt. Dharmasiddha) of Tibetan tradition.[20] A number of his translations from Chinese into Tibetan have been incorporated into the Tibetan canon. Unfortunately, later editions of the canon organize the Dharma in more complex ways than, for example, the ninth-century datalogue of Ldan-dkar (pron. Den-kar) and fail to preserve the simple distinction of Sanskrit versus Chinese origin for each text; with the ethnocentrism peculiar to Tibetan culture they generally fail even to credit Chinese authors or translators.[21] Works done from Chinese have thus had little effect as a class upon Buddhist scholarship in Tibet, except inasmuch as the specifically Ch'an point of view represents an extreme to be avoided—the fallacy that meditative concentration (samādhi) equals wisdom (prajñā).

The Tun Huang school of Fa Ch'eng emphasized not Ch'an, however, but late Mahāyāna scholasticism (perhaps, no different in essence from the lesser-vehicle nitpicking rejected by the school in its early days), and this harmonized with the form of Buddhism that was developing in Tibet. Among the finds at Tun

Huang are seven volumes of notes on Fa Ch'eng's lectures on the *Yogācārabhūmi.*[22] His translation of the *Twenty Verses* fits this context. This translation has been studied by Ueyama from the manuscript collection of the Tōyo Bunkō. The author of the text is given, at the beginning, as "Candragomī-nāma-bodhisattva" (in Chinese), and the translator as tripiṭaka-translator Dharma-master (i.e., ācārya) Fa Ch'eng. Ueyama demonstrates that the translator utilized the *Yogācārabhūmi* translation of Hsüan Tsang and the Tibetan translation of the *Twenty Verses* that is incorporated into the sacred canon. In comments that agree with our own findings, Ueyama dates Candragomin ca. 570-670, and speculates that Śāntarakṣita brought the *Twenty Verses* with him to Tibet for the training of the first monks.[23]

From this same school of Tun Huang also comes a fragment of what constitutes the beginning of a commentary to the *Twenty Verses* which is otherwise unknown, on the reverse of leaves containing monastic prātimokṣa. The Tibetan translation of the *Verses* is basically the same, but this rendering contains errors.[24]

Back in Tibet, roughly half the *Twenty Verses* (vv. 8-16), again in the official translation, are embedded in the *Lo-paṇ bka'-thang* (pron. ka-thang) book of the *Bka'-thang sde-lnga* (pron. de-nga, redacted ca. 1347), perhaps dating from the Early Spread, in a discussion of the three vehicles (śrāvaka-, prateyakabuddha- and bodhisattva-yāna).[25] In this early period the system of Asaṅga and Candragomin is the only guide to bodhisattva practice, although during the Later Spread it is rivaled by the system set forth by Śāntideva (eighth century) in the *Śikṣāsamuccaya.*[26]

Bodhisattva and prātimokṣa vows form a point of controversy between Indian and Chinese parties during the Early Spread. According to the *Bka'-thang,* the Chinese monk named Mahāyāna, a partisan of Ch'an, taught the disregard of moral vows (from the point of view of ultimate truth) in opposition to the teachings of the preceptor Bodhisattva. In the Tibetan representation of this view, morality is regarded as a source of bondage to saṁsāra and inactivity as the path to buddhahood.[27] This is contradicted by the evidence of Tun Huang. The monk Mahāyāna claims in his own defense to have given the "vow of renunciation"—i.e., the prātimokṣa—and the discipline of the bodhisattva to his disciples, and the king (btsan-po) Khri-srong lde-btsan (pron. Ṭi-song de-tsen) is said to have received the bodhisattva vow from a Chinese monk.[28]

Two later commentaries to the *Twenty Verses* are known: from India, that of Bodhibhadra (0 no. 5584), which through his pupil Atīśa (tenth–eleventh centuries) was an influence upon the Later Spread, and from Tibet, that of the Sa-skya (pron. Sa-kya) scholar Grags-pa rgyal-mtshan (pron. Drag-pa gyä-tsen, A.D. 1147-1216).[29] The *Twenty Verses* is also utilized in other Indian and Tibetan discussions of the subject, although matters become complicated by the division of bodhisattva vow lineage into those of Asaṅga and Śāntideva. A detailed exploration of the subject is forthcoming in the form of an annotated translation of Tsong-kha-pa's commentary to the "Chapter on Ethics," the *Byang-chub gzhung-lam* (pron. chang-chub zhung-lam). Notes to the present translation are drawn from various Indian and Tibetan sources.

Confession

Among the works of Candragomin, the *Praise in Confession* (deśana-stava, bshags-pa'i bstod-pa) comes closest to autobiography. In it, Candragomin has taken the verse genre of praise (stava, stotra) and combined it with the religious practice of confession (deśana). The result is a mode, as the commentator puts it, of "praising after confession."[30]

Praise of the Buddha provides the framework of the piece, the bulk of which is devoted to the author's account of the problems encountered in his spiritual practice. The poem constitutes an application to his own life of the principles outlined by Candragomin in the *Twenty Verses*; it corroborates the assertion of Tāranātha that he devoted himself to the bodhisattva path in thought and deed as well as in his writings.

In the *Praise*, Candragomin makes a tour through the list of six perfections, concentrating his attention on his failings in morality (his relationships with others) and in meditation (his attempts at self-improvement). In the course of this pilgrim's progress he explores the various Buddhist practices of his day. Continually overcome by defilement, he perseveres in meditation until confronted by the dead end of Hīnayāna (verse 36), seeing through the illusion of "self" and about to enter the extinction of nirvāṇa. His practices become fruitful only with the discovery of the thought of awakening (bodhicitta), the focal point of Mahāyāna practice. With this discovery he combines the eradication of defilement, both manifest and potential, with the right understanding of reality, and makes rapid progress through the stages to buddhahood. Eventually (v. 50), he identifies himself with the object of visualization—the Buddha—and, himself purified by the process of confession, is implied to have reached awakening. Thus confession functions as catharsis and culminates in mystical experience.

Buddhaśānti, the commentator, is unfortunately not a direct disciple of Candragomin; he is probably a century removed.[31] He claims to have written his "line by line" commentary (vṛtti) at the behest of Sumati, who is otherwise unknown.[32] Although the commentary shows him to be skilled in poetics and in elucidation of doctrine, he makes little effort to relate Candragomin's verse statements to events of his life. Rather, the commentator places himself at a more respectful distance. Addressing himself to the author's motivation for writing (after v. 19), he explains Candragomin's method of self-criticism as an exercise in demonstrating the confession of faults for the benefit of others:

Here, the master's consideration is this: "Even for those who are adorned with many hosts of virtuous qualities and identified with the higher course of conduct, there is a definite place for self-criticism. If and when they have committed an unwholesome deed, whether out of a lack of discrimination or under the influence of an unwholesome adviser, the means for purging it is self-criticism."

Alternatively, one may understand this as introducing others to the confession of fault, by way of thus demonstrating the method . . .

Self-disparagement is a common conceit of the genre of praise, serving to illumine the qualities of the subject. Nevertheless, the *Praise in Confession* is perhaps unique in Indian literature for its forthrightness. Śāntideva's confession in the *Bodhicaryāvatāra* (ch. 2) is quite vague, being really the outline for confession. Perhaps Candragomin, a member of the laity, felt more free to risk losing the appearance of righteousness. The work may have been written early in life, before his separation from wife and in-laws, for in one place (verse 12) he alludes to the hindrance posed by attachment to relatives.

Both the praise and its commentary are written in kāvya style. The poem is terse and epigrammatic, abounding in alliteration, allusion and ambiguity, each verse meant to appear a jewel in itself.[33] The commentary as well, although its task is to connect, to elaborate and to explain, is itself complex and allusive. The two works are aimed at the Buddhist literary set; they combine the imagery of classical kāvya with Buddhist technical terminology. Śāntideva draws heavily upon it in the much simpler *Bodhicaryāvatāra.*

Although one might dare to differ with the commentator on the interpretation of some lines, he may be considered to represent the same philosophic viewpoint as the author. Neither the *Confession* nor its comment adopts a sectarian stance. Criticism of the other Buddhist schools is implicit, however, as the protagonist attempts to make progress by techniques and approaches characteristic of them. In two places (5, 35-36) he reviews the doctrines of the disciples (śrāvakas), discovering their aims to be far distant from altruistic bodhicitta. The Mādhyamika is likewise inadequate because of its division of practice into two "levels" (8): developing its contemplation of emptiness as the relativity of all things, he has no desire to exert himself for the sake of others, and when relying upon the relative level of truth, he grows attached to those same things as being "real."

The terms to which Candragomin subscribes are "balance," "integration" and "the middle way" between the various parts of religious endeavor (31-33). The key to integration is the thought of awakening. Awakening (bodhi) is identical to mystic intuition (jñāna); nonconceptualization (akalpanā) is the means by which to attain it (37c). To develop nondifferentiation one needs faith in and effective practice of the Buddha's teaching, which emanates from his physical form, and a comprehension of it, which constitutes his Dharma form. This last represents the valid intuition of emptiness and the only reality (49).

The process of purification that must be undergone before the attainment of liberation is described as a transmutation (parāvṛtti) of the essential nature of mind. Although "mind is by nature pure and luminous," it has been polluted by adventitious defilement (33d). The reconversion of mind to its original pure state is described with alchemical imagery. The thought of awakening (bodhicitta) is the philosopher's stone, which transforms the base metal of defiled thought into the gold of perfect gnosis (43bcd).

Only one school is mentioned by name in these texts. In response to a friendly objection from the Cittamātra standpoint, the commentator, while not denying its aptness, identifies his own party, for practical purposes, as the Sautrāntika (37d). In fact he belongs to the Sautrāntika-Yogācāra. The former is taken as basis for the examination of phenomena and karmic process—in short, as the valid abhidharma. But this examination is a means to the practice of yoga, with bodhicitta as the key.

Emphasis is placed in the need for teachings to conform to reason (to be "relevant," yukta) in order to be effective. They must accord with logic (hetu) and with the authoritative standards of knowledge (pramāṇa). This is a hallmark of the Yogācāra; one of Candragomin's surviving works is a "defense of logic" along the lines laid down by Asaṅga and Sthiramati.[34] Yet reasoning is subservient to the mystic intuition, gnosis, that comes of successful study and practice (45abc).

No statement of doctrine is made. Among the three svabhāvas of the Cittamātra system, only the second, abhūtaparikalpa, is mentioned by name (40ab). Validity is to be determined by practical experience, and the *Confession* is intended to appeal to readers of all schools.

The commentator makes a few literary references. Dharmakīrti is cited with a verse from the *Pramāṇa-vārttika* (13d). The* *Lavaṇa-nadī sūtra,* otherwise unknown, is quoted on three occasions (2,3,9d). There are two brief citations from other Cittamātra scriptures (37d, 40ab). The doctrine of all these corresponds to that of the *Laṅkāvatāra.* The classical epics are twice alluded to (31a, 37d), and thus the commentator places himself within Indian literary tradition, yet clearly distinguished as a Buddhist paṇḍita.

The *Confession* and its commentary have been preserved by the efforts of Rin-chen bzang-po (pron. sang-po), dean of Tibetan translators. He translated the *Confession* in consultation with the Indian preceptor (upādhyāya) Buddhākaravarman, and its *vṛtti* with Buddhaśrīśānti, also titled "preceptor."[35] Minor differences can be discerned between the text of the *Confession* itself and the version of it that appears in the commentary, most of which can be considered as corruptions.[36]

Rin-chen bzang-po is also responsible for the initial translation of the *Bodhicaryāvatāra*. He is known as a lotsāva whose efforts were capable of improving upon the original. In this case he can be observed at least to have improved upon the *Mahāvyutpatti* and other manuals of translation. His lines flow smoothly and with euphony; many puns and etymological plays are preserved and some new ones introduced. This translation is a model for the rendering of a complex kāvya piece, especially in regard to the limitations of Tibetan vocabulary and grammar vis-à-vis Sanskrit.[37]

Although Candragomin has become a less familiar figure in recent centuries, due in part to the debilitation of Sanskrit studies in Tibet and the narrowing there of philosophic vistas to include only a few Indian texts, it is possible through the translation of Rin-chen bzang-po to catch a glimpse of one of the most vital periods of Buddhist literature in India.

The edited Tibetan texts are available in the author's dissertation, which may be obtained in microfiche from the National Library of Canada, Ottawa K1A ON4 (Canadian Theses Divisions, No. 40796).

Acknowledgments

The translations presented herein form portions of my doctoral dissertation (degree granted by the University of British Columbia in 1978). The research upon which the dissertation is based was carried out on a junior fellowship from the Shastri Indo-Canadian Institute, in affiliation with Magadh University, from October 1975 through March 1977. Dr. Upendra Thakur, Chairman of the Department of Ancient Indian and Asian Studies at Magadh University, graciously extended the aegis of his scholarly repute and personal influence to make my work there possible. With Dr. Artsa Tulku (A-rtsa sprul-sku IX, Bstan-'dzin zla-grags chos-kyi rgyal-mtshan, Dge-bshes Lha-rams-pa of Se-ra) I read the *Twenty Verses* and commentarial literature by Śāntarakṣita and Tson-kha-pa. His patience, perseverance and ingenuity of explanation make him a rare and precious mentor. Beyond that, the hours spent in conversation at his home opened new vistas to me and more than anything else give warmth to my memories of India.

The commentary to the *Twenty Verses* by Grags-pa rgyal-mtshan was read in full with Mkhan-po A-pad (pron. khen-po a-pä) of the Sakya Lama's College (sa-skya'i bshad grwa) then in Musoorie, U.P., with the assistance of his student, Mig-dmar tshe-ring (pron. mi-mar tsë-ring). Later, parallel Sanskrit passages of the *Bodhisattva-bhūmi* were compared with the *Twenty Verses* and with the commentary (in Tibetan) of Śāntarakṣita, and these Sanskrit passages were read with Dr. Leon Hurvitz, who consulted the Chinese version of the *Bhūmi* (Hsüan Tsang translation) at many points.

The texts were edited, by-and-large, at the Library of Tibetan Works and Archives at Dharamsala, Himachal Pradesh. Geshe Ngawang Dhargyey (dge-bshes-ngag-dbang-dar-rgyas) of that institution lent his assistance in negotiating a number of difficult passages of the *Praise in Confession*. It is a pleasure to thank the director of the Library, Mr. Gyatsho Tshering, for placing its resources at my disposal, and the then-secretary, Mrs. Kesang Takla, for making my stay there most comfortable.

Dr. David Seyfort Ruegg made helpful comments on the translation of the *Praise in Confession*. Dr. Leon Hurvitz made numerous suggestions for improvement of its style.

Notes to the Introduction

1. Kalupahana, David W., "Concept of a Person in Early Buddhism" (unpublished).

2. Dayal, Har, *The Bodhisattva Doctrine in Buddhist Sanskrit Literature* (repr. Delhi: Motilal, 1975).

3. There has been speculation by Sukumar Dutt, recapitulated by Charles Prebish, that the *prātimokṣa* refers originally to a formal expression of faith rather than to the recitation of rules. But this is based upon the failure to comprehend crucial terms in early glosses of *prātimokṣa*—for example, *kṣepaṇa,* which has Dutt at a loss but indicates "prescribed, artificial (morality)." See Prebish, "The Prātimokṣa Puzzle: Fact versus Fantasy" (*Journal of the American Oriental Society* 94.2, 1974), p. 169a.

4. According to the vinaya of the Mūla-Sarvāstivāda. For the enumerations of other schools see Prebish, ibid., and R. F. Sherburne, "A Study of Atīśa's Commentary on his Lamp of the Enlightenment Path" (Ph.D. dissertation, University of Washington, 1976), p. 230, n. 54 and 233, n. 56.

5. Translated by Mark Tatz as "The Vow of Benevolent Conduct (Bhadracari)" in *Studies in Indo-Asian Art and Culture,* vol. 5, pp. 153-76 (New Delhi: International Academy of Indian Culture, 1977).

6. On the date of Candragomin see the article of that title by M. Tatz in *Buddhism and Jainism,* part 1, pp. 281-97 (Cuttack: Institute of Oriental and Orissan Studies, 1976), and Chapter One of the same writer's "Candragomin and the Bodhisattva Vow" (Ph.D. dissertation, University of British Columbia, 1978).

Lists of Candragomin's works appear in M. Hahn, *Candragomins Lokānandanāṭaka* (Wiesbaden: Harrassowitz, 1974), pp. 10-11, and M. Tatz, "The Life of Candragomin in Tibetan Historical Tradition" (*Tibetan Review* 6.3).

7. zhi ba lha dang tsandra go mi la// rmad byung slob dpon gnyis zhes rnams sgrog. Tāranātha, *'Phags-yul chos-'byung* (Sarnath, 1971). Cf. translation by Alaka Chattopadhyaya, *Tāranātha's History of Buddhism in India* (Simla: Indian Institute of Advanced Study, 1970), p. 18.

8. J. Takakusu, *A Record of the Buddhist Religion as Practiced in A.D. 671-695, by I-Tsing* (London: Oxford, 1896), p. 164.

9. sdom la gnyis la gnas pas gzhan gyi don btang ste/ bdag gi don lhur len par rig par bya'o// Otani no. 5583, Peking Bstan-'gyur Ku 203a.

10. Ibid., 204b.

11. Chapter Six of Candrakīrti's *Madhyamakāvatāra* contains his extensive refutation of a Cittamātra opponent.

12. kye ma 'phags pa klu sgrub gzhung// la la'i sman la la la'i dug// mi pham 'phags pa thogs med gzhung// skye bo kun la bdud rtsi nyid// (Tāranātha, op. cit. 148.3-4; tr. p. 205).

13. Otani no. 3534, *Bhagavad-ārya-mañjuśrī-sādhiṣṭhāna-stuti.*

14. Otani no. 4489, *Śrī-mahā-tārā-stotra.* Details on the painting and the praise appear as an anecdote in the Sde-dge and Snar-thang editions of the Bstan-'gyur: *Candragomyākhyāna* (btsun-pa zla-ba'i gtam-rgyud).

15. See A. K. Warder, *Indian Kāvya Literature,* vol. 2 (New Delhi: Motilal, 1974), index s.v. ambiguity.

16. Bu-ston, *History of Buddhism,* tr. E. Obermiller (Heidelberg: Harrassowitz, 1931-32), vol. 2, pp. 196-97.

17. Ibid., 2.187. For the accounts of other histories see Tatz, dissertation, op. cit., p. 256; n. 117, 118.

18. Bu-ston, op. cit. 2.188, 190. On lay vows being given first see Dpa'-bo gtsug-lag, *Mkhas-pa'i dga'-ston* (completed 1565), ed. L. Chandra from the ms. of T. Densapa, vol. Ta (Lo-paṇ chos-'byung), 90a.7 (New Delhi: International Academy of Indian Culture, 1959).

19. See his phrase "such as a monk" in the ceremony for confession (Tatz, dissertation, op. cit., ch. 5, sect. 3.222) and ibid. 3.231.12 & n. 49, the passage an afterthought. Śāntarakṣita is also credited with a text on monastic ethics (*Ldan-dkar Catalogue* item no. 512, ed. M. Lalou, *Journal Asiatique* 241 [1953], p. 331).

20. Ueyama's research reviewed Demiéville, *T'oung Pao* 1970, pp. 47-62. Chos-grub has sometimes, since his initial identification by Pelliot (JA 1908, p. 513) been mistakenly taken for a Tibetan, e.g., by Lalou (JA 1927, p. 240, n. 1), and it is not always clear in *Le Concile de Lhasa* (Paris: Imprimerie Nationale, 1952: index s.v.) that Demiéville has recognized the identity of Fa Ch'eng and Chos-grub. On his life, ca. 755-849, see Demiéville, ibid., pp. 34-37; TP 1970, p. 49; HADANO Hakukyū in *Acta Asiatica* 1975, p. 89.

21. Only the Sde-dge edition, for example, credits Chos-grub with translation of the *Upāyakauśalya Sūtra.* Some Chinese materials in the canon are reviewed by Tucci, *Minor Buddhist Texts* vol. 2 (Rome: Istituto Italiano per il Medio ed Estremo Oriente, 1958), Introduction.

22. TP 1970, p. 59. see also Li Fang-kuei, "A Sino-Tibetan Glossary from Tun Huang," TP 1963, pp. 233-356.

23. *Indogaku Bukkyōgaku Kenkyo,* vol. 11 (1963), pp. 715-721. This article, in Japanese, was read with the assistance of Shoji Matsumoto.

24. Ms. furnished by the British Museum. See La Vallée Poussin, *Catalogue of the Tibetan Manuscripts from Tun-huang in the India Office Library* (Oxford: University Press, 1962), item no. 633.1. Ed. & tr. Tatz, dissertation, op. cit., pp. 221-225 & n. 107.

25. Gter-ston O-rgyan gling-pa (b. 1323), ed., *Bka'-thang sde-lnga* (Paro: pub. by Ngödup at Khyichu Lhakhang, 1976), 766.3f. On this text and its antiquity see Anne-Marie Blondeau, "Le Lha-'dre Bka'-thang," in *Etudes Tibétaines* (Paris: Libraire D'Amérique et D'Orient, 1971); Tucci, *Tombs of the Tibetan Kings* (Rome: Istituto Italiano per il Medio ed Estremo Oriente, 1950), pp. 39-41; and Vostrikov, *Tibetan Historical Literature,* tr. H. C. Gupta in *Indian Studies Past and Present,* 1970, pp. 226-229, 237f.

26. According to Tsong-kha-pa, Śāntideva combines the system of transgressions of the *Ākāśagarbha-sūtra* with that of the *Bodhisattva-bhūmi* (*Gzhung-lam* 46a.5-47b.3; Tatz, dissertation, op. cit., pp. 201-202).

27. Tucci, *Minor Buddhist Texts,* part 2, op. cit., p. 99; Bu-ston, *History,* op. cit., 2.191-192. On the subject see also Guy Bugault, *La Notion de "Prajñā"* (Paris: E. de Boccard, 1968), pp. 158 n. 1, 159 ("The end of morality in *samādhi,* freedom even from *praṇidhāna* . . . .")

28. Demiéville, *Concile,* op. cit., pp. 162, 164, 220.

29. *Sa-skya-pa'i Bka'-'bum* (Tokyo:Toyo Bunko, vol. 4, 1968), item no. 136.

30. *bshags nas bstod pa* (closing verses).

31. Buddhaśānti (colophon: *sangs-rgyas zhi-ba*) is identified by Tāranātha and others as a disciple of Buddhajñānapāda. He is said to have gained the siddhi of Mañjuśrī in Vāraṇāsī, and of Tārā in Potāla. His fellow student Buddhaguhya had contact with the court of Khri-srong lde-btsan (Tāranātha, op. cit., pp. 276 & n. 8, 280-283). He is not the sixth century Buddhaśānta who visited China and engaged in translation work (*Encyclopaedia of Buddhism* 3.462-463; *Hōbōgirin,* Fascicule Annexe p. 129 [s.v. Butsudasenta]).

32. *blo-gros-bzang-po* (closing verses).

33. On Buddhist *stotra* see A. K. Warder, *Indian Kāvya Literature* vol. 2, op. cit., paragraphs 871f.

34. Candragomin, *Nyāyasiddhyālokā,* Otani no. 5740.

35. Rin-chen bzang-po, A.D. 958-1055, referred to in the colophons as *Zhu-chen gyi lotsāva dge-slong Rin-chen bzang-po.* See Claus Vogel, *Vāgbhaṭa's Aṣṭaṅgahṛdayasaṁhita* (Wiesbaden: Deutsche Morgelandische Gesselschaft, 1965), pp. 20-21 & refs. n. 20. Buddhaśrīśānti arrived in Tibet when Rin-chen bzang-po was age fifty-five. Both Indians are named by the colophons in transliterated Sanskrit and entitled *rgya-gar gyi mkhan-po.*

36. At 31a of the commentary none of the four editions names the epic heroines correctly.

37. For an example of the limitations of Tibetan vocabulary for rendering technical terms see n. 110 to the English translation.

Candragomin's Resolve

Salutations to princely Mañjuśrī:

1. *With anxiety for the karma of existence,*
However and wherever I am born,
In that [form] and in that [place],
Pure in faith and in faculties,

2. *Knowing all crafts and skills,*
Fearless in all treatises,
Turning my back to all desires,
Magnanimous in all matters,

3. *Mindful and speaking truth,*
Cheerful in the sight of sentient beings,
Serving a spiritual adviser
Who is adorned with the thought of awakening,

4. *Endowed with correct, disciplined deportment,*
Mindful of good intellect and clean rebirth,
My course will have a wholesome object,
Out of fear for sinful karma.

5. *Adhering to the ten perfections,*
The supreme and ultimate achievement,
May I become the unwavering protector,
Who brings only happiness to the world.

6. *Let me not become a slave or a female,*
Nor be born a fool, or in a bad area,
Let my future Buddhahood be visible,
And may there never be any wrong views.

7. *Let me become Buddha with a desireless manner,*
Enjoying things that are not desired by others;
Let me not live on alms I may desire,
When they are the cause of distress.

8. *Developing love for sentient beings;*
Not seeking the effect of reaching buddhahood
And awakened mind, the nature of which has no cause.
Born in a high family with intelligence and wealth,
With a handsome form in birth after birth,

9. *Composing poems for many Sugatas,*
Taking on birth upon rebirth,
I will be born in those families
That produce divine Buddhas.

10. *In birth after rebirth,*
Not relinquishing five dharmas—
Merit, gnosis and strength,
Vigor and the thought of awakening—

11. *Just as the all-knowing one,*
Had his means to attain the stage,
So may I, by my own means,
Obtain the stage of the sage's faculties.

Twenty Verses on the Bodhisattva Vow

1. *Make prostration with reverence and offer what you can*
To the Buddhas and their disciples;
Then the moral code of bodhisattvas
Who abide in all time and space—

2. *That treasury of all merit—*
Should be taken, with lofty intention,
From a lama maintaining and learned in the vow,
Who is capable [of bestowing it].

3. *At which time, because of the virtue in that,*
The Jinas and their disciples
With their virtuous hearts, forever
Consider you their beloved son.

4. *For others, as for oneself,*
What is suffering may be beneficial;
Do beneficial pleasant things,
But not the pleasant, if not beneficial.

5. *That which, developed from severe defilement,*
Functions as destruction of the vow,
The four transgressions of it,
Are considered as defeats.

6. *With attachment to gain and respect,*
Praising oneself and deprecating another;
Stingily not giving Dharma and wealth
To the suffering, [poor] and forsaken.

7. *Heedless of another's confession,*
Striking him out of anger;
Rejecting the Greater Vehicle,
And showing what appears like good Dharma.

8. *The vow should be taken again;*
Confess the middling outflows to three,
The rest before one [person],
The defiled and not, in one's own mind thus.

9. *Not offering three to the Precious Three;*
Following thoughts of desire;
Not paying respect to elders;
Giving no answer to questions;

10. *Not accepting an invitation;*
Not taking such things as gold;
Not giving to those who seek Dharma.
Disdaining the immoral.

11. *Not training for the sake of others' faith;*
Doing little for the welfare of sentient beings;
With mercy there is no [deed] without virtue.
Ready acceptance of wrong livelihood;

12. *Laughing aloud, and so on, from levity;*
Thinking to travel only in saṁsāra;
Failing to ward off defamation;
Not to give treatment even comprising affliction;

13. *Abuse in return for abuse, and so forth;*
Disdaining those who are angry;
Rejecting another's excuses;
Following thoughts of anger.

14. *Attracting followers out of desire for honor;*
Not dispelling laziness and so forth;
Giving way with a passion to gossip.
Failure to seek the goal of concentration;

15. *Not to eliminate hindrances in meditation;*
Regarding the taste of meditation a good quality.
Rejecting the auditors' vehicle;
Diligent in it while having one's own method;

16. *Diligent only in outside treatises;*
Taking enjoyment in that diligence;
Rejecting the Greater Vehicle;
Praising oneself and deprecating another;

17. *Not to go for the sake of Dharma;*
Deprecating it and relying upon the letter.
Not being a friend in need;
Refusing to serve the sick;

18. *Not acting to remove suffering;*
Not teaching what is relevant to the careless.
Not to repay a good turn;
Not to assuage the sorrow of others;

19. *Not giving to those who seek wealth;*
Not working the welfare of followers.
Not to conform to the expectations of others;
Not speaking in praise of good qualities.

20. *Not to suppress in accord with conditions;*
Not using psychic powers to threaten and so forth.
There is no fault in a wholesome thought either,
Compassionate and [acting] out of love.

Commentary to the Twenty Verses on the Bodhisattva Vow

Texts referred to *(in order of reference)*:

Bbh. Asaṅga. *Bodhisattva-bhūmi*. Otani no. 5538. Skt. ed. Nalinaksha Dutt, Patna: Jayaswal Research Institute, 1966; and by Unrai Wogihara, Tokyo, 1930. Tib. Peking ed. vol. Zhi.

Dutt, Nalinakṣa, ed. "Bodhisattva Prātimokṣa Sūtra." In *Indian Historical Quarterly* vol. 7 (1931), pp. 259-86.

Śāntarakṣita. *Saṁvara-viṁśaka-vṛtti*. O 5583.

Abhayākara (-gupta). *Munimatālaṁkāra*. O 5299.

Atīśa. *Lam-sgron (Bodhipatha-pradīpa)*. Ed. and tr. R. F. Sherburne. "A Study of Atīśa's Commentary on his Lamp of the Enlightenment Path." Ph.D. dissertation, University of Washington, 1976.

Guṇaprabha. *Bodhisattva-śīlaparivarta-bhāṣya*. O 5546.

Jinaputra. *Bodhisattva-śīlaparivarta-ṭīkā*. O 5547.

Samudramegha (Rgya-mtsho sprin). *Yogacaryābhūmau bodhisattvabhūmi-vyākhyā*. O 5548.

Grags-pa rgyal-mtshan. *Byang-chub sems-dpa'i sdom-pa gsal-bar ston-pa shlo-ka nyi-shu-pa'i rnam-par bshad-pa*. In *Sa-skya-pa'i bka'-'bum*, vol. 4, no. 136. Tokyo: Toyo Bunko, 1968.

Tsong-kha-pa. *Byang-chub gzhung-lam*. O 6145.

Bodhibhadra. *Bodhisattva-saṁvara-viṁśaka-pañjikā*. O 5584.

Verses 1-2 refer to the ceremony for taking the bodhisattva vow. Two preconditions are indicated (*2b-d*): the candidate's intention and the availability of someone else from whom to take the vow. The Bbh says, at the beginning of the "Chapter on Ethics": "Because he has become obligated to morality by someone else, when the bodhisattva transgresses his training, then dependent upon the other a dread of blame (vyapatrāpya) will be born. Because he has a quite purified intention (suviśuddhāśaya), when the bodhisattva transgresses morality [following Tib.], then dependent upon himself a sense of shame (hrī) will be born" (Skt. Dutt 95.11-14, Wogihara 137.18-22; Tib 85a.4-5).

The "lofty intention" with which the candidate approaches the taking of the vow is the aspiration (praṇidhāna) to attain nirvāṇa for the sake of all living beings. With the taking of the vow to attain buddhahood, the "aspiration" aspect of the thought of awakening is transformed into the aspect of "setting forth" (prasthāna), for an actual step has been taken toward fulfillment of the goal. So the candidate must be sincerely motivated by the thought of awakening, and the teacher whom he approaches will test his resolve and intention with suitable questioning.

The "other" from whom the vow is taken must herself or himself have taken and kept the vow and be qualified to impart it. Like the candidate, he may be either lay or monastic. He must have faith in the vow and be of a character that is not in contradiction with any of the six perfections. He must know the ceremony in letter and in spirit and must in addition be an object of reverence for the candidate. In the absence of a suitable party from whom to take the vow, it may be taken by oneself before an image.

The actual ceremony consists of a question and affirmation:

Thereupon, he [the candidate] should be addressed thus: "Will you, kulaputra so-and-so, receive from me all the bodhisattva bases of training and all the bodhisattva ethical codes—the ethic of the vow, the ethic of collecting virtuous dharmas, and the ethic of accomplishing the welfare of sentient beings—whatever the bases of training and ethical codes of all bodhisattvas of the past, whatever the bases of training and ethical codes of all bodhisattvas of the future, and whatever the bases of training and ethical codes of all bodhisattvas presently abiding in the ten directions may be—whatever the bases of training and ethical codes in which all past bodhisattvas have trained, all future bodhisattvas will train, and all present bodhisattvas are training?"

And he must affirm, "Yes, I will."

The learned bodhisattva should speak so a second and a third time, and when asked, the recipient bodhisattva should, all three times, affirm it.

(Skt. Dutt 105.25-106.9, W 153.24-154.13, Bodhisattva-prātimokṣa-sūtra *[ed. N. Dutt] 2a.4-b.3; Tib. 94a.4-b.1; Śāntarakṣita 194a)*

The three ethical codes of the bodhisattva named here represent the three-part classification of bodhisattva praxis of the "Chapter on Ethics." "Bases of training" (śikṣāpada) are the particulars of practice and known from reason and from scripture; they are in fact conceived as infinite (see Abhyākara, *Munimatālaṁkāra* 93.lff.; Atīśa, *Lam-sgron,* p. 261).

The ceremony concludes with an announcement by the teacher to the buddhas and bodhisattvas of the present time that the candidate has joined their ranks. The new bodhisattva is warned against rashly publicizing his status to the uninitiated, who may be hostile to the Mahāyāna, lest his taking of the vow incur demerit instead of merit. Then he is taught the bases of training and the bases of offense against the vow, as they are set forth in the Bbh (see below).

The bodhisattva vow is a "treasury of merit" especially by comparison with the prātimokṣa vow obligation, for it aims at universal liberation.

(These two verses summarize part of the section on the vow of the "Chapter on Ethics" of the Bbh: Skt. Dutt 105.7-107.10, W 152.22-156.3; Tib. 93a.8-95a.8. For commentary and variants see Śāntarakṣita 193a-195b; Guṇaprabha 234b.4-235a.3; Jinaputra 253b.8-255b.3; Samudramegha 196b.7-198a.8; Bodhibhadra 213b.3-228a.2; Bodhibhadra, *Bodhisattva-saṁvara-vidhi* [O 5362, 5404]; Atīśa, *Cittotpāda-saṁvara-vidhi-krama* [O 5403, 5364]; Jetāri, *Bodhicittotpāda-samādāna-vidhi* [O 5406, 5363]; Grags-pa rgyal-mtshan 4a.1-12b.5; Tsong-kha-pa 30b.6-36a.1.)

Verse 3. The vow is considered to have been effectively transmitted when the buddhas and bodhisattvas give a sign of acknowledgment, such as an earthquake (Jinaputra, Samudramegha, Tsong-kha-pa). The teacher's announcement has then reached them by direct mental cognition (jñāna-darśana). (Bbh Skt. Dutt 106.18-107.2; W 154.27-155.17, *Bodhisattva-prātimokṣa-sūtra* [ed. Dutt] 4b.1-3; Tib. 94b.6-95a.4. See also Śāntarakṣita 195b-196a; Guṇaprabha 235a.3-4; Jinaputra 254a.8-b.6; Samudramegha 197b.7-198a.4; Bodhibhadra 228a.7-b.5; Grags-pa rgyal-mtshan 11b.4-12a.4; Tsong-kha-pa 35b.1-6. On *jñāna-darśana,* Pāli ñāna-dassana, see Guṇaprabha, Jinaputra, Samudramegha ibid.; MHV nos. 151-53; VM 20.2, 22.119; AK 7.27c-28 & n. pp. 193-94; PTSD s.v.; K. N. Jayatillike, *Early Buddhist Theory of Knowledge* [London: Allen & Unwin, 1963], pars. 718ff.)

Verse 4 begins the main part of the work, on keeping the vow or fulfilling bodhisattva conduct, by presenting the general rule. The bodhisattva must deduce for himself what is fitting to do and what is not fitting, and he must also follow the teachings of the Buddha as set forth in the scriptures and systematized in the Bbh. In general, he should do what is pleasant and beneficial for others, but when a contradiction presents itself, he should sacrifice present pleasure for long-term benefit, as a doctor will give bitter medicine or a person will avoid eating sweet pudding that has been poisoned.

At this point the Bbh merely directs the student to reason and to scripture. The contrast of benefit and pleasure would appear to be original to Cg; it forms a starting-point for the later *Śikṣāsamuccaya* of Śāntideva, the first pada of which is identical (see also BCA 8.95-96).

(Bbh Skt. Dutt 107.10-14, W 156.3-9; Tib. 95a.8-b.3. On reason and scripture see Jinaputra 255b.3-6; Samudramegha 198a.8-b.3; Tsong-kha-pa 37b.7-39a.8. On benefit versus pleasure see Bodhibhadra 228b.5-229a.6; Grags-pa rgyal-mtshan 13b.1-5; Tsong-kha-pa 39a.8-b.5.)

The remaining verses unfold the particulars of keeping the vow. *Verses 5-7* deal with contradictions severe enough to destroy the vow. As with the monastic prātimokṣa vow, there are four such "defeats." But unlike defeat (pārājika) in the monastic system (unchastity, murder, theft or spiritual boasting), which results in the perpetrator being barred for life from monastic status, the commission of bodhisattva defeat (pārājayika) can be rectified by retaking the vow. Hence the bodhisattva equivalents are "considered as [being like] defeats" (*5d*). Furthermore, in order to cause him to lose bodhisattva status the transgression must be committed with "severe defilement" (*5a*), in that it is committed with four elements of obsession (paryavasthāna): regularity, lack of conscience, a sense of satisfaction and a view for its advantages. If committed with middling or lesser obsession, the deed becomes a "misdeed" (duṣkṛtā).

Cg does not mention that another cause for relinquishment of the vow is relinquishment of the aspiration for supreme awakening (Bbh Dutt 109.13-15). According to Śāntarakṣita, this is because it is so obvious (197a).

So long as the aspiration has not been relinquished nor any defeat been committed, the vow cannot be lost even upon the bodhisattva's death and subsequent rebirth. In this also the bodhisattva vow differs from that of the monk. Even if the vow is not remembered in his next lifetime, receiving it then is considered a mere refreshment of memory. Needless to say, the bodhisattva vow may not be voluntarily relinquished, as may monastic vows, for to give up monastic vows will disappoint only one's own hopes for liberation, but to give up the bodhisattva vow breaks a promise to the whole world (Tsong-kha-pa; see also BCA 4.5-6, 9-10).

The four bodhisattva defeats are described in *vv. 6-7*. Each has two elements, which has led some later commentators to list them as eight. (This is discussed by Tsong-kha-pa.)

(Bbh Skt. Dutt 108.11-109.20, W 158.2-160.9; Tib. 96a.6-97a.7. See also Śāntarakṣita 197b-198a; Guṇaprabha 235a.4-236b.4; Jinaputra 256b.8-259a.2; Samudramegha 199b.5-201b.4; Bodhibhadra 229a.6-233a.2; Grags-pa rgyal-mtshan 14b.5-17a.3; Tsong-kha-pa 42a.7-43a.4, 54b.3-57b.5; 61b.3-62b.8.)

Verse 8 indicates the sorts of ceremony for dealing with "defeat" and "misdeed" types of offense. In the case of defeat (with greater degree of obsession) the vow must be taken again. Here the Bbh presents the ceremony for taking the vow by oneself. A deed of "defeat" done with middling obsession must be confessed before three Buddhists (not necessarily bodhisattvas). Those of lesser obsession should be confessed to one person. The misdeeds listed below, classified as "defiled" and "not defiled," may be confessed mentally, the bodhisattva resolving that it will not happen again.

(Bbh Skt. Dutt 109.8-12, 124.11-125.7; W 159.16-23, 180.22-182.4; Tib. 96b.8-97a.3, 108b.1-109a.4. See also *Bodhisattva-prātimokṣa-sūtra* [ed. Dutt] 4b.4-4a.2; Śāntarakṣita 198a-199b; Guṇaprabha 236b.5-237a.1; Jinaputra 258a.5-8, 272b.2-273a.1; Samudramegha 200b.8-201a.3, 214a.3-214b.2; Bodhibhadra 228a.1-2, 233a.2-235b.6; Grags-pa rgyal-mtshan 12b.6-13a.4, 17a.4-18a.5; Tsong-kha-pa 36b.4-37a.3, 57b.5-58a.4, 86b.1-87b.1.)

"Misdeeds" proper are generally numbered at forty-six and classified in two sets: thirty-four that contradict the bodhisattva ethic of collecting virtuous dharmas, and twelve that contradict the ethic of working the welfare of others. The first set unfolds according to the order of the six bodhisattva "perfections" (pāramitā). So *line 9a* begins the subset of seven misdeeds contradictory to giving (dāna): failing to make daily offering of body (for example, act of prostration), speech (recitation of a verse) and mind (an act of faith) to the Precious Three (Buddha, Dharma and Community). In case of mere forgetfulness, distraction, etc., the fault is not defiled. Among the other extenuating circumstances, Bbh notes that "for one who has reached the stage of purified intention (śuddhāśaya-darśanamārga, pramuditābhūmi [Tsong-kha-pa 64a.2-3; *Siddhi* 603, 729; AK 5.6, Samudramegha 203a.2; CPT s.v. *aveti*]) there is no fault, for such a bodhisattva has a purified intention—just as the bhikṣu who has advanced to 'faith through understanding' (avetya-prasāda) is always serving the Teacher the Dharma and the Community by the nature of things, and doing worship with the highest offerings."

The six perfections are covered by the following lines of verse: giving, *9a-10c;* ethics, *10d-12d;* patience, *13a-d;* vigor, *14a-c;* meditation, *14d-15b;* and wisdom, *15c-17b.*

(Bbh Skt. Dutt 109.21-120.19, W 160.10-175.18; Tib. 97a.7-105b.4. See also Śāntarakṣita 199b-209b; Jinaputra 259b.8-271a.5; Samudramegha 202b.1-212b.7; Bodhibhadra 236a.2-246b.8; Grags-pa rgyal-mtshan 18a.5-25b.2; Tsong-kha-pa 63a.5-81a.4.)

By being avaricious and discontented the bodhisattva also contradicts giving (*9b*). By paying no respect to elders or refusing to answer a question, he fails in the giving of confidence (*9cd*). By not accepting invitations or even money (*10ab*) he fails to make himself a basis for another's merit of giving. Most importantly, he must not fail in the giving of Dharma (*10c*). As always, there are extenuating circumstances, such as mental upset, and the generally applicable distinction between defiled failure, when the deed is committed with malice, and undefiled sins of omission.

In the discussion of ethics (śīla), the moral code of the bodhisattva is distinguished from that of the monk. To begin with, it is the bodhisattva's concern to harbor special compassion for the violent and immoral, as opposed to those who are peaceful and easy to deal with (*10d*). Beyond this, he must follow the "common" prescript, the lifestyle ordained by the Vinaya for monks, for if monastic deportment creates faith in those who observe it, how much more so must the bodhisattva conduct himself as a good monk "for the sake of others' faith" (*11a*). Nevertheless, he must not adhere to those monastic prescriptions that prevent him from accomplishing great deeds for the benefit of others (*11b*). For example, he may collect money and requisites more than he needs for himself, in order to distribute them to others, although to do so breaks the monastic rule. Finally, he may (or should—the point is not clear) rise above not only prescribed codes of ethics, but natural morality as well. So he will slay an individual who is about to commit a mass murder, taking the karmic consequence upon himself, overthrow (steal the power of) a tyrannical king, cohabit in adultery, lie and commit slander, speak harshly, and indulge in idle speech—which signifies the composition of theatrical entertainments and so forth (*11c*).

The last point, countenancing apparent immorality in the bodhisattva, has been noticed by La Vallée Poussin ("Le Vinaya et la Pureté d'Intention" in Académie Royale des Sciences, des Lettres et des Beaux-Arts de Belgique, vol. 7 [1929], pp. 210-17). The qualification is that the bodhisattva does so with skill in means (upāya-kauśalya)—with a purified intention and with a thought of mercy in his mind.

Lines *11d-12a* adduce failures in livelihood (the coercion of donations, etc.) and in deportment which, in common with the monk, he must avoid. *12b* alerts him to the danger of misinterpreting the stance of the bodhisattva vis-à-vis nirvāṇa and saṁsāra. The bodhisattva does indeed forego the entry into nirvāṇa and instead remains in saṁsāra to assist other beings. But this is not to say that he does not strive to eliminate the defilements that stand between him and nirvāṇa, or that he somehow "enjoys" the state of saṁsāra.

The bodhisattva must dispel bad reports of himself (*12c*), but he must not be loath to resort to severity when it will result in benefit for sentient beings (*12d*).

Under contradictions to patience (kṣānti) we have, firstly, the ancient set of four "dharmas of the śramana": returning abuse for abuse, anger for anger, blow for blow and cavil for cavil (*13a*). The bodhisattva must turn aside others' anger toward himself by apology or appropriate excuse (*13b*) and must himself demonstrate forbearance, never rejecting another's excuses (*13c*) or harboring resentment (*13d*).

Contradictions to vigor (vīrya) are comprised by inferiority of physical, mental and verbal activities: attracting a following for the material reward, not dispelling laziness, and the indolence of gossip and social intercourse (*14abc*).

Contradictions to meditation (dhyāna) are subsumed under preparation, principle and goal: to fail to seek instruction, to fail to eliminate hindrances to meditation (excitedness and regret, ill will, drowsiness and languor, sense-desire, and doubt), and to become distracted by the enjoyment of trance states (*14d-15b*).

Finally, eight points contradict wisdom (prajñā): to reject the auditors' vehicle (śrāvaka-yāna) as beneath study for the bodhisattva or, on the other hand, to study it to the exclusion of the bodhisattva collection of sūtras (*15cd*); to study non-Buddhist arts and sciences to the exclusion of Buddhist or to overly enjoy what diligence in them is appropriate (*16ab*); to reject something incredible or not understood in the Mahāyāna (*16c*); self-praise and deprecation of others (*16d*); to disdain going to hear a preaching or to deprecate the preacher by referring to the letter instead of to the meaning (*17ab*).

The second set of misdeeds comprises twelve that contradict the obligation to work the welfare of others.

(Bbh Skt. Dutt 120.20-124.3, W 175.19-180.10; Tib. 105b.4-108a.5. See also Śāntarakṣita 209b-212b; Jinaputra 271a.5-272a.6; Samudramegha 212b.7-213b.7; Bodhibhadra 246b.8-249b.6; Grags-pa rgyal-mtshan 25b.2-28a.5; Tsong-kha-pa 81a.4-84a.5.)

Generally, there is (1) the fulfillment of need, in which regard the Bbh mentions establishing what beings require, being a traveling companion, providing employment, guarding property, reconciling differences and meritorious deeds (*17c*)—and (2) the alleviation of suffering: serving the sick (chief among those who suffer), removing suffering in general and correcting those embarked upon a wrong course, for this is the cause of suffering (*17d-18b*).

There are two categories of misdeed in connection with particulars: failure to render assistance and failure to suppress others' misbehavior. The former includes ungratefulness, lack of commiseration, ungenerosity, failure to attend to the needs of one's followers, failure to be sociable and in accord with social expectations, and failure to praise good qualities (*18c-19d*). As to the latter: he should punish those who deserve punishment, humiliation or banishment (*20a*), and use his wonder-working powers to frighten those who deserve it (*20cd*).

As with all misdeeds, there are extenuating circumstances, including incapacity and the pursuance of a higher aim. Nor is there fault in any deed done with compassion (*20cd*). In general, says the Bbh, citing scripture, "Know the faults of the bodhisattva to be for the most part developed from aversion, rather than from desire-attachment."

(The scripture thus cited is noted identified, but Grags-pa rgyal-mtshan and Tsong-kha-pa refer to the *Upāli-paripṛcchā,* for it agrees in sense with paragraphs 42 and 43 of that text [Python tr.]. See also the *Upāyakauśalya-sūtra,* cited *Śikṣāsamuccaya* [Skt. 93.12-17, tr. pp. 163-64]. On *20cd* and the generalities of extenuation see Bbh Skt. 124.3-11, 125.8-13, W 180.10-22, 182.5-14; Tib. 108a.5-b.1, 109a.4-7. See also Śāntarakṣita 212b-213a; Jinaputra 272a.6-273a.6; Samudramegha 213b.7-214b.6; Bodhibhadra 249b.6-250a.7; Grags-pa rgyal-mtshan 28a.5-28b.4; Tsong-kha-pa 84a.5-89b.3. See also La Vallée Poussin, "Bodhisattva," in James Hastings, ed., *Encyclopaedia of Religion and Ethics,* vol. 2 [N.Y.: Scribner's, 1918].)

Praise in Confession

Salutations to princely Mañjuśrī!

1. *Peerless king of physicians, guru of the world,*
Totally faultless one, source of virtuous qualities,
Having visualized you, O refuge, I, always ill,
Shall confess, describing my changes of fault.

2. *Like an extremely hard to cross ocean current,*
With waves of sordid discursive preoccupation,
When agitated by the sharks of defilement,
My mind has not been made calm.

3. *Tossed by great waves of the sea of desire-attachment,*
If I rely on the vessel as unclean,
There my mind, by the fire of aversion,
Is burned off and destroyed like dry grass.

4. *To pacify the scorching fire of aversion,*
Even if I develop the lotus pond of love,
There, wishing happiness for all people,
The mind ends in the mire of attachment.

5. *To purify the stains of the mire of attachment,*
If I cleanse it with the water of evenmindedness,
There even the World-protector's compassion,
Which dispels the distress of all creatures, would decay.

6. *O Chieftain, if I cultivate compassion,*
Great sorrow is generated in me;
If I rely on gladness to pacify this,
The distracted mind grows excited.

7. *If I produce sadness to calm that joy,*
There mind will grow helplessly depressed;
Persistently praising the inferior,
I come within range of the enemy conceit.

8. *I cultivate all-emptiness, the antidote to that,*
There I have no effort for the sake of others;
If I resort to the relative for their sake,
There the wish for wealth is born.

9. *If I set the mind to amassing wealth,*
I ferment the liquor of all the faults;
Drunk, drowsy with pride and delusion,
All higher aims end only in defeat.

10. *Even when I may wish to give,*
Powerful stinginess restricts me
But even if I dispel it and come to give,
For a long time after I regret it.

11. *Making myself serene with faith in a future reward*
Becomes a fall into the fruits of the next world;
If I act without expectation, aware of impermanence,
Without a motivation I dissolve in apathy.

12. *Protector, I am torn by the suffering of the world,*
Viewed as having been relatives even in the past;
I wish to course in the welfare of others,
But am held in check by having the notion of "self."

13. *On the tracks of the view of self follows conceit,*
Which makes me embrace "mine";
There conceit, pride, desire and so forth
Shatter me like angry enemies.

14. *When the net of defilement is all unfolded*
And frightening as the legion of Māra,
Like the unendurable mark of time
The darkness of sinister directions spreads.

15. *I will recite my misdeeds; the regret to follow is hard to support;*
Rebirth would be suffering unendurable;
What oppression is greater than that?
I myself course the same way.

16. *When I turn away from harming others,*
Which acts as the cause of the various sufferings,
Having become an enemy to the blameless wretched crowd,
I shake at it with violence like the edge of a sword.

17. *Even when I wish to make myself patient,*
I am tied by their binding misconduct;
Terribly blocked and tied by that,
The fire of aversion dries me of all sympathy.

18. *Just as vipers, unbearable to see,*
Dwelling within a tree repel the wise
So concealing a course of hatred,
My attitude repels virtues.

19. *Like a stone [slab] baked by sunshine,*
Like clods become dust by dehydration,
Like a road filled with heaps of sand,
The rain of Dharma is no benefit in my mood.

20. *My own unbearable suffering uninvestigated,*
Someone such as tries to do me a favor,
Who helps me with forbearance and generosity,
That, O World-protector, I am unable to bear.

21. *Hating him or fleeing and evasive,*
Highly unsettled or repelling him—even so,
He instructs those like me unceasingly;
Even so, I do not think of him as a guru.

22. *Even having gone to request, it is hard to find;*
At a time for patience, the best, the great medicine,
If I am not patient with a patient disposition,
What other occasion for patience will I have?

23. *Held by demonic defilement, their minds are agitated;*
Feverish, they cannot even try to help themselves;
As I observe the world, worthy of my regard,
O Chieftain, aversion is born, but nothing of compassion.

24. *People course in the fruits of their own activity,*
Aware of the inevitable dissolution of all;
Having even examined the blamelessness of others,
See their projections out of foggy confusion!

25. *I myself, though an ocean of faults,*
Do not tolerate even a fraction of someone [else]'s;
I count patience a blessed quality in another,
But for this I am not patient—here's the wonder!

26. *As though rising into the springtime sky,*
Masses of cloud defilements in my mind
Come and go again and again;
Unabashed, I am wretchedly apathetic.

27. *But even if the cold wind of defilement has come to arise*
And been zealously defeated with a blaze of concentration,
With the spreading smoke of drowsiness and languor
Desires for a bed proceed to grow.

28. *My mind is rendered helpless by the noose of desire-attachment,*
Burned by the fire of aversion, conquered by the conceits;
All filled with weapons, the arrows and the spears
Of all the faults, I am helplessly stupefied.

29. *Finding my memory, bound and soon atremble,*
Crushed, I am dissolved;
Lured by pretense and delusion
I circle through the lower range of Māra.

30. *Whatever, however I envisage for the calm state,*
Focusing, refocusing the mind there upon it,
From this the noose of defilement
Drags me helpless toward objects with the rope of attachment.

31. *If I tend to diligence, excitedness ensues;*
Relinquishing that, depression is produced;
Its proper balance being difficult to find,
What shall I do for my agitated mind?

32. *Coursing in wisdom, excitedness will emerge;*
Holding to restraint, depression will be born;
Its integration being difficult to find,
What shall I do for my agitated mind?

33. *Proceeding with perseverence, excitedness will result;*
Relaxing that, depression will be born;
Its middle way being difficult to find,
What shall I do for my agitated mind?

34. *Over and over, with the forest fire of meditation,*
The jungle of fault may be burned, yet
The fixed root of "self" being unconsumed,
It comes to life in advance, as though moistened by rain.

35. *For some the flux of mere defilement-karma-fruition,*
By being seen, will be diverted;
Do they not eliminate even the flow of thought?
This is quite far from interest in the welfare of the world.

36. *The guardians part only from attachment,*
Regardless of all the world;
The flow of thought, like a lamp whose cause is exhausted,
Enters nirvāṇa, the remaining aggregates consumed.

37. *Whatever dispels the distress of all the world—*
The thought of awakening: ambrosia, elixir—
When I develop the nonconceptual as cause of awakening,
Then I am only chasing differentiations.

38. *All the world is like a dream—by no one*
Is there any act of perception whatsoever;
Even having cultivated, I course in the very range
Of the enemy: differentiation of conceiver and conceived.

39. *O Chieftain: this quite unendurable hurt—*
Observe it and grant me the immaculate view;
Whatever I cherish, whatever preoccupies me,
Those very things frustrate me at the start.

40. *But what can the Lord do for faults*
That I myself have created before?
The dispeller of darkness for all the world, the very sun
Cannot dispel the black darkness of those who have been
born blind.

41. *Relying for so long upon what is unhealthy*
And having constant mental infatuation with it,
I am punished with leprous hands and feet;
What can I do by occasional reliance on medicine?

42. *The tree of thought, from beginningless ages of time,*
Moistened and fostered by the bitter sap of defilement,
I cannot make a sweet tasting substance of it;
What will it become with a drop of quality water?

43. *My mind has all the faults by its very nature;*
Great wonder should awakening become the philosopher's stone!
Even as I apply myself to just that quality,
I continue to be the very substance of fault.

44. *Whatever is taught as the great medicine itself,*
Just that becomes poison for me;
Were there a better elixir which were relevancy itself,
If I have no confidence, it does not truly exist.

45. *Whatever dispels certain more intense defilements*
And does not cause the production of others,
That is called "relevant"; being in my mind,
How then has it not been made certain as well?

46. *The impressions of predisposition, tendency, and element—*
Applying myself to the antidote for [these] causes of fault—
When I develop the instructions for meditation,
Here, before long, they grow calm.

47. *O Guardian, completely devoid of all faults,*
Who sees the highest meaning of all dharmas,
By expounding it in various modes as well,
You entirely dispel the seeds of defilement.

48. *Your body blazing with marks of beauty,*
As I see the presence before me,
So I come to hear the nectar drunk by ear;
The seeds of defilement are entirely destroyed.

49. *O Chieftain, you are far superior to that,*
Possessing also the supreme sun of the Dharmabody;
Even with meditation, it eludes the range of the world—
That it conquers the fog of fault: What a great wonder!

50. *With whatever high mind is appropriate,*
Abiding in whatever calm state is appropriate,
Who pacifies all the faults in all the modes,
Whatever the Lord may be, that I salute.

51. *By the virtue of framing a proper praise*
Of such confession to the supremely qualified one,
Whatever I have gathered, bright like a beautiful moon,
May everyone go to the Land of Bliss.

Commentary by Buddhaśānti to the Praise in Confession

Salutations to princely Mañjuśrī!

Now, while making praise, he addresses himself to the exhortations, beginning from a three-pointed situation characterized by the Buddha as cause, effect and fulfillment of purpose. There are also three points [to be made here] regarding the author of a praise: his faith, erudition and arrival at some situation of anxiety.[1]

So this [first verse] depends chiefly upon a situation that has created a need, occasioned by erudition. Out of a desire to speak in the manner of confessing misdeeds, and by way of describing the qualities of the Lord [bhagavat], he says:

1. *Peerless king of physicians, guru of the world,*
Totally faultless one, source of virtuous qualities,
Having visualized you, O refuge, I, always ill,
Shall confess, describing my changes of fault.

The "king of physicians" is the chief physician, because he is learned in the science of healing sentient beings who are afflicted by the disease of the defilements and go to lower states of rebirth.[2] For that reason, he is "peerless." Among such [deities] as Brahmā and Rudra, there does not exist one who is his equal in technique.[3]

Furthermore, being the teacher of the highest path to those of the triple realm, he is "guru of the world."[4]

"In that view, would not the auditors and independent buddhas also be considered 'gurus of the world?'"[5] In order to distinguish [the Buddha] from them, he says "totally faultless one." "Faults" refers to desire-attachment, aversion, bewilderment and so forth, for these create obstacles to the growth of right intuition (jñāna) in one's stream of thought. He is freed from them all without remainder, together with the impressions [that give rise to them]; they have been abandoned.[6]

By merely being faultless, has one become a guru? To that he says, "source of virtuous qualities." As it must be trained and refined, it is a "virtue." The implication is that, in having fashioned [qualities] such as power and courage, he is their "source," the basis for their production.[7]

Being worthy as a refuge for these reasons, [the author says] "refuge": resorting to which, the negative alternatives—misdeeds and so forth—are consumed. Possessing the personal greatness (mahātmya) of extraordinary qualities, the Lord Buddha is the foremost refuge. So he is addressed as "refuge."

"You" have become an object of visualization by direct cognition.[8] "Having visualized": having envisaged and made you evident with a mind of absolute faith. One might add: "I shall confess my faults."

Why confess? "[I am] always ill." This should be taken as affliction by the disease of defilement and possession of the characteristic of grasping at "I" and "mine," not as being shaken by (diseases of) wind and so forth. For this is not the situation.[9]

"My changes of fault" indicates that his own mind has weakened in its essential nature under the sway of defilement and that there are methods for changing this into some other situation. The sense is that "I will make confession—speak openly, without dissembling—with a reverent manner of spoken terms and of body: palms joined and so forth."

So this first verse is [intended] to demonstrate, as his own duties, the subject matter, the connection, the purpose and the further purpose. Confessing his own faults by way of describing the qualities of the all-knowing one himself is the "subject matter," while the terms of praise are the description. Their connection as cause and effect is the "connection." To turn away from defilement, by way of knowing the path, is the "purpose." The gradual attainment of the rank of buddha that depends upon it is the "further purpose."[10]

To show those changes of fault regarding himself (vv. 2-11), he says:

2. *Like an extremely hard to cross ocean current,*
With waves of sordid discursive preoccupation,
When agitated by the sharks of defilement,
My mind has not been made calm.

"Oh Lord! My mind has not been made calm and free from defilement."

In what way is it not so? "Like an extremely hard to cross ocean current."[11] "Like" introduces a simile. The sense is that just as those carried off and unsettled by the strong current of a river experience great suffering, so he, being unsettled by the hard to reverse flood of defilement [that flows] through the state of saṁsāra, has not made his mind calm and at ease.

Because of what? "With waves of sordid discursive preoccupation." By application [to objects], one has "preoccupation" (vitarka), the grosser motion of thought. By [their] detailed investigation, one has "discursiveness" (vicāra), a mode of mental precision.[12] What is preoccupied and discursive is sordid as well —so "sordid discursive preoccupation," possessed of defilement.

Those are the waves. The mind in a state of being agitated and unsettled by modes of defiled preoccupation and discursiveness is "possessed of waves." Hence it is "hard to cross."

Again, what is it like? "When agitated by the sharks of defilement." Under the influence of sordid discursive preoccupation have been produced the defilements, beginning with desire-attachment (rāga). These are "sharks"—the marine animal—inasmuch as they grasp firmly and create suffering in a like manner. There are "hosts" of them—many.[13]

For that reason, as long as defiled preoccupation has not been cleared up, one's mind will not become calm and a basis for the growth of bright/wholesome dharmas.

As is explained in the *Salt Sea (Lavaṇa-nadī) Sūtra:*

I have no fear for robbers who [may wish to] steal my wealth,
For if they once should steal my good wealth, it cannot happen
again;
But the wealth of mental virtue, well gathered again and again,
[Is always] openly stolen by my vulgar preoccupations.

In mountain caves, in cellars or in the depths of the forest
I can secure this wealth from robbers;
But wherever I may go with the wealth of virtue,
There is no land unconquered by ignoble preoccupation.[14]

The Buddha has taught, for those possessed of desire-attachment, aversion and bewilderment, [meditations upon] the unclean, love and dependent origination respectively. In order to show that a situation has resulted that is out of harmony with His promulgation of the four stations of brahma (brahma-vihāra), and [addressing himself] specifically to the first of those [defilements, the author] says (vv. 3-7):

3. *Tossed by great waves of the sea of desire-attachment,*
If I rely upon the vessel as unclean,
There my mind, by the fire of aversion,
Is burned off and destroyed like dry grass.

"Desire-attachment" includes desire for sexual love and desire for [other] things.[15] Being great and powerful, it is a "sea." Its "waves" are the manifold differentiations (vikalpa) associated with it. Tossed and distracted by them, he has become troubled.

And as the same sūtra explains:

Just as serene Watercourse Ocean[16]
Is greatly shaken by waves,
So the water of one-pointed thought
Is disturbed by differentiation.

When one has become this way, what should be done? One

should rely on the antidote. So he says, "If I rely on the vessel as unclean." If, to seek [the antidote],[17] he develops unclean repulsive things, relying upon the vessel as a means of crossing the ocean of desire, and so remains . . .

What is the mind like, remaining in that condition? "There my mind, by the fire of aversion/ Is burned off and destroyed like dry grass." In that condition of meditative development, under the influence of reliance upon unpleasant objects, his mind is burned like dry grass by the fire of aversion, while he does not find the peace of mind of being freed from desire, which was itself harmful to the mind. Thus the description of his own fault.

Granted that such aversion is harmful. What if he relies upon its own antidote? To this he says (v. 4):

4a. *To pacify the scorching fire of aversion,*

"Aversion (dveṣa) is the intention of harming another—a form of enmity (āghāta). This is the fire. Scorched by the unhappiness arising from it, the mental continuum is incinerated.

"Peace" means [putting] that harm at peace,[18] turning away from that trend of thought.

"To" means "for the sake of that." What does he do for the sake of calm?

b. *Even if I develop the lotus pond of love,*

Although he develops, as antidote to the fire of aversion, friendly and loving thoughts, wishing happiness for all sentient beings, which [thoughts] are cooling like the waters of a lotus pond and able to douse the fire of aversion, and although he makes much of it . . .

What comes of this?

c. *There, wishing happiness for all people,*

There, in the state of meditating thus, with loving thoughts "for all people"—for those of the world comprised by the triple realm, without exception—he wishes for the envisioned happiness and [develops] harmless, affectionate thoughts.[19]

When the mind is thus focused, what ensues?

d. *The mind ends in the mire of attachment.*

When he wishes happiness with loving thoughts, then a craving desire, connected with a thought for its gratification, comes to be born. And that [desire], since it constitutes a state of mental settling (niveśa) or sinking, is a "mire." Thus the mind comes to be exhausted.

This is being shown: When one acquires an attachment to creatures by means of loving thoughts combined with strong affection, that is a fault.

Even so, how does one progress? To that he says:

5a. *To purify the stains of the mire of attachment,*

"Attachment (saṅga) means clinging to things (vastu-abhiniveśa). Since it functions as the cause of saṁsāra, it is like a mire. It is a stain: the deepseated problem of settling down in "I" and "mine."

What should be done to purify and purge such stains?

b. *If I cleanse it with the water of evenmindedness,*

That attachment, which is like a mudstain, should be understood as a fault on the part of the intellectual faculty of understanding (prajñā-mati). When he cleanses it—dispels the stains—with water-like evenmindedness, free from approval and resentment, and [so] has no regard for any creature, what fault ensues?[20]

cd. *There even the World-protector's compassion,*
Which dispels the distress of all creatures, would decay.

O World-protector! In that condition—placed in evenmindedness—even the great compassion that functions as the protector and refuge of the world, working to dispel the suffering of all creatures by extricating (them from saṁsāra), by engagement in worldly affairs (avatāraṇa), would decay and become nothing. Hence I would be no bodhisattva.

But what if he also contemplates compassion itself?

6ab. *O Chieftain, if I cultivate compassion,*
Great sorrow is generated in me;

"Chieftain" is a vocative.

If, having seen that problem, he develops and actualizes compassion itself, then everywhere is born the great mental affliction known as "sorrow." "Alas! These sentient beings are everywhere defiled by suffering." The sense is that the mind becomes very afflicted by sorrow, thinking in this way.

What should be done for that?

c. *If I rely on gladness to pacify this,*

If he relies upon and comes to remain in the station of brahma termed "gladness" in order to pacify the affliction proceeding from compassion and to maintain a balance, what follows from that?

d. *The distracted mind grows excited.*

When he directs the mind toward joyful things, then under the influence of glorifying the mind that is distracted toward objects, that is ever changing, he only becomes excited and puffed up; he does not dwell in a natural peace.

There must be some other reliable means by which to pacify this.

7ab. *If I produce sadness to calm that joy,*
There mind will grow helplessly depressed;

Having envisioned such saddening things as the aspects of suffering in order to calm the mind proud with joy, sadness is produced. In that condition, by reason of the very production of sadness, the mind grows depressed in subservience (to it). The sense is that, in its inability to focus on the meditative image, it is enfeebled in effort.[21]

If, having become so, he enthusiastically glorifies it, what fault ensues?

cd. *Persistently praising the inferior,*
I come within range of the enemy conceit.

And if he should, with persistence and perseverence, glorify [this] depressed, inferior mood in any way so as to make of it a matter of pride a fault ensues. Why? He has come within range of the enemylike conceit, excessive conceit and so forth, which conquer his wealth of virtue.[22] He comes under their sway. The sense is that he has become a slave of the nemesis known as "conceit."

Having thus shown the mental problems that ensue when he envisions the four stations of brahma, he now shows what problems ensue when resorting to the antidote to conceit.

8a. *I cultivate all-emptiness, the antidote to that,*

In order to dispel that nemesis "conceit" he develops the engagement of mind that functions as its antidote, the "all-dispelling, all-emptiness"—emptiness that annihilates all things, animate and inanimate. With it one comes to reverse all negative alternatives such as conceit, just as mutually exclusive characteristics such as darkness and light [dispel one another], or as do physical objects characterized by dwelling separately, such as jar and blanket. In this case he dispels the [notion of] separately dwelling physical objects and works to develop the meaning of emptiness.[23]

Even cultivating the meaning of emptiness in this way, what ensues?

b. *There I have no effort for the sake of others;*

In that condition of cultivating all-emptiness, because he neither envisages himself nor sentient beings [in general], he has no diligence or perseverance in the work of maturing other creatures, [not to speak of] the welfare of the world. The sense is that "I am diverted from that."

With such a problem, how should one envision? To which he says:

c. *If I resort to the relative for their sake,*

For the sake of dispelling that problem of the view of emptiness, he relies upon and maintains "the relative," which constitutes an obscuration to seeing the right meaning; he relies upon dharmas that function as things (vastu).[24]

What further problem comes from that?

d. *There the wish for wealth is born.*

Applying his thought thus to things he generates the attitude of earning and increasing wealth by any means, by trading and so forth, and with that his mind becomes afflicted and defiled. Because, when one relies on the relative, wishing to send gifts and so forth, there is born the idea of hoarding the various objects of wealth such as gold and jewels.

What fault is there in having thus generated the attitude of accumulating wealth?

9a. *If I set the mind to amassing wealth,*

Having produced a craving for wealth, he relinquishes his special application to meditation and so forth. Then, if he sets his mind to amassing or collecting [items of] wealth such as gold, generating a craving for it, the mind has come under the sway of distortion (viparyāsa). Therefore,

b. *I ferment the liquor of all the faults;*

"When I borrow from others I grow careless; faults of physical defilement and so forth will proceed." [In other words], by that one fault is fermented or produced, like alcohol, for the person guarded by his wealth, the cause of [further] fault.[25]

What further faults will ensue?

c. *Drunk, drowsy with pride and delusion,*

For those reasons the mind is not aware of the distinction between what should and should not be done. So it has been made "drunk."

With what is he made drunk? "Drowsy with pride and delusion." Like a drunkard he is proud, his intellect weakened by arrogance and delusion; he has come under the sway of drowsiness and languor. Due to "pride" he has "delusion," while with "delusion" he grows drunk with drowsiness.

From these what fault proceeds?

d. *All higher aims end only in defeat.*

Whatever might be accomplished presently and in future lives by excellence—in other words, all higher aims (abhiprāya) that act as the cause of exaltation and sublimity—is defeated and pulverized.

"Only" marks a restriction.

In short, the meaning here is this: He craves the accumulation of wealth, and that is the cause of faults such as the abuse of others.

Again, from the *Salt Sea Sūtra:*

All that reverence and good qualities
It annihilates;
Though they be heavy as Mount Meru,
It makes them light as cotton wool.

With craving, in wintertime,
Not even Himālayan cold,

Nor in blazing desert sunshine
Can the heat be felt.

With craving a bottomless ocean
Of anxiety for many sorts of harm
Is thought to be very small,
About the size of the track of an ox.

Having thus shown the way in which his mind is unbalanced, in order to show further that his thoughts stemming from the accumulation of wealth are uncongenial with sincere giving itself, he says (v. 10):

10ab. *Even when I may wish to give,*
Powerful stinginess restricts me,

"At whatever time I may wish to make gift of my hard-earned wealth and to share it out to beggars, even then 'powerful stinginess'—clinging to things, and the total bondage of attachment-creating stinginess associated with the power of beginningless ages of time—these two 'restrict me': I am rendered powerless to renounce (anything) by their firm hold on my intellect."

What should be done then? He says (10cd-11d):

cd. *But even if I dispel it and come to give,*
For a long time after I regret it.

Having dispelled—that is, eliminated—that stinginess by virtue of developing the antidote alternatives, he has come to give certain things to certain individuals who constitute the field [for giving]. Nonetheless, afflicted anew by thoughts arisen from stingy craving, for a long time he regrets the renounced objects.

Even if he turns his thought from that by relying upon conviction what ensues?

11a. *Making myself serene with faith in a future reward*

"Faith" (śraddhā) is mental serenity (citta-prasāda). With belief and with faith that aspires to virtuous qualities, he has dispelled the stains of his mind. Made cleansed and serene, however,

b. *Becomes a fall into the fruits of the next world;*

The sense is that clinging even to the fruits of having renounced material objects and expecting some return, the mind becomes dis-integrated.

When dis-integrated in that way,

c. *If I act without expectation, aware of impermanence,*

Recollecting the word of the Teacher: "All formations are impermanent," he examines the various modes of impermanence.[26] By means of that antidote, making him aware that material objects and so forth have no permanence, but are modes of momentariness,[27] he has detached himself from the expectation of a return, from enjoyments and so forth that might develop as the karmic maturation of giving. But even when he has dispelled that mental pollution, things do not go well. Why?

d. *Without a motivation I dissolve in apathy.*

Since by giving gifts as the cause, one should obtain a corresponding great enjoyment as the result,[28] there is cause for perseverance in giving and so forth, which function as causes for the accomplishment of such results. The implication is that, in order to rid himself of the expectation of a result, he has lost the desire to make effort in dharmas such as giving, and his mind, under the sway of apathy, is only dissolved and dejected, becoming enfeebled.

Having demonstrated confession in describing his failure with regard to his own welfare (2-11), in order to show further what acts as a fault in terms of the welfare of others, he says:

12a. *Protector, I am torn by the suffering of the world,*

O Protector! I am torn—that is to say, distressed—by reports of the three or eight sufferings—the suffering of the formations and so forth or that of birth and so forth—of this world of sentient beings.[29]

They are also

b. *Viewed as having been relatives even in the past;*

During his succession of previous lives in this state of saṁsāra, he has been related to others as to parents and so forth. He intellectually views them as having been connected with himself; he imagines it.

"Even" means "not only in the present."

With that as cause, what does he do?

c. *I wish to course in the welfare of others,*

Since sentient beings hardpressed by suffering are not unrelated [to himself], he wishes to course in the bodhisattva career, working the weal of others by giving and so forth in order to dispel their oppression. But when he undertakes to fulfill that duty, what ensues?

d. *But am held in check by having the notion of "self."*

From the mental impressions (vāsanā) of "relatives" and so forth, there develops the notion of "I" and "mine," by which he is "held in check" or ruled. The sense is that there ensues the distortion of viewing a "self" in what is [really] self-less.[30]

What is likewise near the view of self?

13a. *On the tracks of the view of self follows conceit,*

The view of self is the assertion that the so-called "self" truly exists. To fancy a self in the selfless is "conceit." That conceit follows upon the view of a "self." The sense is that he comes to settle down in tīrthika views such as permanence, stability and the existence of a self.[31]

And what fault is produced by them?

b. *Which makes me embrace "mine";*

He is bound by this mistake that has developed from conceit, for it occasions the growth of a firm embrace of the idea of "mine," or "by me."

What mass of faults does having become so produce?

c. *There conceit, pride, desire and so forth*

"There": while in that condition in which there grows an embracing of "mine." Then faults of conceit and so forth are produced.

"Conceit" refers to the faults of "conceit," "excessive conceit" and so forth.

"Pride" means a full-blown and vainglorious mind.

"Desire" means sensuality,[32] by which is produced a craving for objects of attachment.

By saying "and so forth" he includes the other defilements, such as aversion and bewilderment. And what do they do?

d. *Shatter me like angry enemies.*

As when hostile enemies are enraged, they instigate many sorts of harm such as depriving one of life, so also those masses of defilement steal the life of virtue and instigate the various sufferings of change.[33]

Therefore the view of self is the basis of all faults. As the master (ācārya) Dharmakīrti has explained:

If there exists a self, there is the notion of other;
From the self and other pair, come embracing and aversion;
In connection with these two,
All faults are generated.[34]

To show some similes for the negative alternatives produced by those same faults of conceit and so forth, he says (*14*):

14ab. *When the net of defilement is all unfolded*
And frightening as the legion of Māra,

"When . . . legion of Māra": Māra is the ruler of the realm of sense-desire;[35] his legion is an armed host. And because they, brandishing various weapons, show no decency in entering into battle or dispute, they are much to be feared.

"As" denotes similarity, for in actuality he is frightened by the production of masses of defilement and various sorts of harm.

"Defilement" indicates desire-attachment and so forth, while "net" should be taken as "great hosts of them." Or, he is tied up and bound by his total ensnarement in them. Such defilement has spread everywhere;[36] it stimulates his latent tendencies (anuśaya) toward sense objects.[37] When blazing in all its aspects of total ensnarement in defilement, the mass of defilement itself constitutes a legion of Māra. So the blazing impact of unbearable defilement is

c. *Like the unendurable mark of time*

"Time" is the messenger of the Lord of the Dead.[38] The "mark of time" is that he wishes, some nighttime, to tie people with a lasso round the neck and carry them off.[39]

"Like" denotes similarity, on the model of the net of defilement: The resemblance is that it generates quite unendurable fear. "Like that,"

d. *The darkness of sinister directions spreads.*

The faction (paksa) of Māra—the darkness of delusion, acting as the opposite to bright/wholesome dharmas—spreads and increases. Alternatively, "dark/sinister directions (pakṣa) may be taken as the waning face of the moon.[40] If, within its gloomy darkness, certain enemies should bring down a rain of weapons, one would be very frightened. The sense is that, by analogy, while he is obscured by the darkness of defiled directions, sundry harms and sufferings come to spread.

By thus showing various modes of simile, he has demonstrated that the mass of defilement proceeding from the view of a self is much to be feared. For that reason he wishes to confess, by way of criticizing his misdeeds, in order to pacify it:

15a. *I will recite my misdeeds; the regret to follow is hard to support;*

O Lord! I will recite before you the many sorts of misdeeds that I have committed; whatever misdeeds I have accumulated for the sake of the pleasant and unpleasant both—I will cause them to resound.

Why? "The regret to follow is hard to support." Whatever I have done, the train of regretful thought subsequent to it, with its potentiality for renewed existence, is hard to support, hard to bear, for that [regrettable] rebirth will have the same nature as the misdeed.[41]

Why again?

b. *Rebirth would be suffering unendurable;*

"Rebirth" means taking on a physical form in accord with one's destiny. "Suffering" indicates that [this form] will have the nature of being five aggregates (skandha).

"Rebirth . . . suffering" refers to the suffering of rebirth.[42] As he has come again and again to take it on—to grasp it—the suffering of change that develops from activity (karma) and defilement is produced and willingly experienced: This is what is unendurable. The sense is that there will certainly be produced various mental and physical sufferings that will be very hard to support.

So,

c. *What oppression is greater than that?*

By way of a rhetorical question: "What thing could there be that is more greatly oppressive than the suffering that has developed from defilement?" More precisely: "There is nothing at all more oppressive than that."

As to having thus understood that unendurable suffering has a cause, whereas it would be relevant (yukta) to remove it, he has not done so; rather,

d. *I myself course the same way.*

He confesses, by way of describing his own fault, that "Although I may have grasped that there is a cause of suffering, I myself personify the course of misdeeds that acts as its cause, rather than reversing it, and this is to have come under the sway of defilement."

If that be the case, is it not appropriate (yukta) to turn one's thought from that, eliminating [the cause]? That is so, but he is incapable of patience,

16ab. *When I turn away from harming others,*
Which acts as the cause of the various sufferings,

In line with this, tolerance is the wellspring of all pleasure, whereas anger acts as the basis of all suffering. So the latter attitude is said to "act as the cause of the various sufferings"; it is aversion that acts as the cause and basis of the aspects and varieties of suffering, in this and the next world, that proceed from the body-mind complex, because from it emerges injury to sentient beings.

By reasons proceeding from resentment, he harms others and causes suffering. When he turns his thought from that by way of recollecting the faults of anger and, by recollecting the antidote [as well], makes himself tend to patience . . .

What happens in such a state?

cd. *Having become an enemy to the blameless wretched crowd,*
I shake at it with violence like the edge of a sword.

His intellect, incapable of tolerance, is shaken, and the flow of thought polluted.

How so? "Having become an enemy to the blameless wretched crowd. . . with violence like the edge of a sword." The crowd, those deprived of the higher course of morality, patience and so forth, have become wretched by nature. He has unreasonably become their enemy; he lacks even the basis for blame that they have done him harm. Violent and cutting like the edge of a sword is he toward the conduct of those he has come to detest—so, "my thought shakes."

What if he should nonetheless resort to tolerance even for those who are wretched by nature, and attempt to sympathize with them?

17ab. *Even when I wish to make myself patient,*
I am tied by their binding misconduct;

At whatever season or moment he has turned his mind from that disturbance and brought about mental serenity by means of the antidote, even then if he wishes to establish himself in a patient mode, at that time his thoughts are tied and bound firmly once more to those whose own minds are bound, to the wretched nature of those naturally wretched opponents and to the various types who behave so as to cause various sorts of harm. The sense is that he thus comes under the sway of aversion.

Even so, why does he not retract his thought, fixing it in evenmindedness regarding their behavior?

cd. *Terribly blocked and tied by that,*
The fire of aversion dries me of all sympathy.

While forcefully blocked and tied by that bond of aversion that has developed from their wretched behavior, he does not maintain a flow of thought that is excessively patient: He has come under the sway of annoyance. Hence the terrible aversion arisen from that [misbehavior], because it scorches himself and others, is like a fire. That fire, because it robs the mind of the moisture of the noble Dharma, is said to dessicate the mental continuum. So with it his mind has become "devoid of sympathy," without compassion. The sense is that he is deprived of patience and serenity for the higher course of conduct.

What is his state of mind like, thus deprived of sympathy (*18*)?

18a. *Just as vipers, unbearable to see,*

"Just as" introduces a simile. "Vipers, unbearable to see" refers to a certain snake that is able to kill merely by being seen. The venomous breath can stupefy one.[43]

b. *Dwelling within a tree, repel the wise,*

The one tree hollow in a thousand that is inhabited by such a venomous serpent instantly repels the wise (paṇḍita), the intelligent (dhīmat), [even] at a great distance.

cd. *So concealing a course of hatred,*
My attitude repels virtues.

This statement shows the point of the simile. In the same way, "hatred"—the course of harming others—developing from the venomous, serpentlike share of aversion, is like venom in that it is concealed, abiding within; it is "my hypocritical attitude."[44] Mind in this aspect is like the tree; it is here shown to be rejected or abandoned by "virtues": by groups of activities (karmāṇi), such as the three trainings, that function as the causes of exaltation and sublimity.[45]

The sense is this: If the course of aversion, associated with enmity, abides like a snake in one's mind, it [the mind] is a virtual repository of venom and virtuous dharmas will not last; they will be repelled.

To illustrate again, how on account of deepseated psychological problems he fails to become a repository for the Dharma, he says, ". . . by sunshine . . . the rain of Dharma is no benefit in my mood."

In what way?

19a. *Like a stone [slab] baked by sunshine,*

Like rain falling on a slab of stone that has been baked and scorched by the hot, keen rays of the summer sun . . . . "Like" indicates resemblance: "Just as" a stream of rain may have fallen onto the face of a rock, but no growth, sprout, etc. appears; it will neither be wet inside nor even a bit moist outside, and nothing will appear on it even for an instant.

Likewise his mind, scorched by hundreds of defilements fierce like rays of the sun, derives no benefit from the rain of Dharma.

Again, what is it like?

b. *Like clods become dust by dehydration,*

Just as a heap of clods, baked[46] and totally dried out by the sun's rays, turns to dust—like clods of earth in a very rough state—and just as rain may have fallen on these dried and roughened piles of clods, but nothing different is born of them, nothing of benefit . . . .Although they may have been a bit moistened by enough of a downpour, they will remain so until the next season.[47]

In a like manner, when one's mind has been dried and turned to dust by the hosts of sordid differentiation of beginningless ages of time, the rain of Dharma brings no benefit.[48]

Once more, what is it like?

c. *Like a road filled with heaps of sand,*

"Heaps of sand" means sand piles; the sense is "a great deal." "Filled" means covered over and screened by them. Rainfall on a frequented road in that direction is of no benefit.[49]

"Like" makes a simile. Just as rain may have fallen in streams enough on a road filled with heaps of sand, accomplishing nothing useful, for it soon continues as it had been before . . . .

Similarly,

d. *The rain of Dharma is no benefit in my mood.*

The rain of right Dharma into a reservoir such as my mind, already filled with sandy ignorance, craving and so forth, is of no benefit.

The similes show this: "Rainfall on good fields has the benefit of causing the growth and prosperity of crops and grains such as fruit. The back of a stone, a heap of clods and a sandy road, on the other hand, are unlike this." Thus he demonstrates [his point] with dissimilitude.

The three similes mentioned may be applied to his lack of benefit from having relied upon the three aspects of Dharma respectively: scriptural tradition, personal discovery and the ultimate reality.[50] Alternatively, they may be taken to apply to the several collections (piṭaka) of Dharma teachings of the three vehicles respectively.[51]

Here the master's consideration is this: "Even for those who are adorned with many hosts of virtuous qualities and identified with the higher course of conduct, there is a definite place for self-criticism. If and when they have committed an unwholesome deed, whether out of a lack of discrimination or under the influence of an unwholesome adviser, the means for purging it is self-criticism."

Alternatively, one may understand this as introducing others to the confession of fault, by way of thus demonstrating the method; and by virtue of the mortification, he has become freed from misdeeds. For it is explained that "Even having committed a quite intolerable misdeed, one may banish it by self-criticism."

This method is adaptable to other situations as well.

Showing the method of self-criticism again to others,[52] he says (*20-21*): "My own suffering . . . ." "Their benefit as well, O World-protector," invoking the Lord, "that also I am unable to bear." There is the additional sense that "I am not only without reverence for the path that you have shown and without its benefit, but I have also been unable to know and rely upon yourself."

Why so?

20a. *My own unbearable suffering uninvestigated.*

The fierce and rugged masses of suffering that I myself experience—unbearable, hard to support—because they have developed as the maturation of [my own] misdeeds, have not been intellectually investigated and recognized." For that reason,

b. *Someone such as tries to do me a favor,*

"Someone such as" yourself, acting as a close friend, who interests himself in what is beneficial to me and turns away what is harmful . . . .Alternatively, "such as" may be interpreted as drawing not a comparison but a restriction: whether "the very one who is interested in my welfare," or "one whose function is to try to do me a favor."

How?

cd. *Who helps me with forbearance and generosity,*
That, O World-protector, I am unable to bear.

"Forbearance" refers to the perfection of patience, "generosity" to the perfection of giving. These two [among the six perfections], being the foremost means of helping another, are mentioned at the head. The sense is that there are, among the best of them, [some] with the disposition to help and fulfill one's needs. But when they exhibit those two [traits], he cannot bear it; he cannot rely upon it.

"What do I do; [how am I] unable to cope?"

21a. *Hating him or fleeing and evasive,*

"Hating" means forming the notion of him as a nemesis.

What else does he do? "Fleeing and evasive." When given beneficial advice, unable to bear it, he goes elsewhere.

b. *Highly unsettled, or repelling him—even so,*

Not taking the advice, he wanders at random; he directs his thought someplace [else]. Or else, "repelling him": Even if there is a remaining in place, he verbally repels [the other], abusing him.

"Even so" introduces a very difficult mode. [The other] teaches—he bestows the rain of good Dharma upon—even those who have become so unfortunate by being so intractable, so troublesome, their trend of thought so disinclined to it. "Even for those as unfortunate as I and so wretched by nature . . . ."

cd. *He instructs those like me unceasingly;*
Even so, I do not think of him as a guru.

He instructs continuously, initiating them to knowledge (vidyā) and bringing them fortune [i.e., giving them the opportunity].[53]

"[Even] so": Although that may be the case, "I fail to think of him as being a guru who gives beneficial advice." The sense is that he misconstrues, because the mind's eye has been blinded by ignorance.

This is being shown: Just as those born blind are ignorant of the shapes of the sun and moon, so likewise sentient beings who have not developed the body-mind continuum are incapable of discovering the meaning of the profound Dharma; they cannot take beneficial advice.

Having thus spoken to the changes of his psychological problems (*1-21*), now, to show how to entreat the Lord with a true, original mind, he says (*22*):

22a. *Even having gone to request, it is hard to find;*

"Having gone": As though there were an occasion for assistance and the eager recipient has "gone" straight for it; he has then done honor and so forth; he has made his request, but it is very hard to find, hard to obtain, and,

bc. *At a time for patience, the best, the great medicine,*
If I am not patient with a patient disposition,

Whenever his injured mind has been wounded by an angry opponent, there is a need for healing with the technique of a cheerful acceptance of suffering and so forth. Hence at that time he needs to rely upon patience, because patience is the reliable medicine, the most distinguished of all means, "great" in that it heals mental illnesses. In [this need is implied] a patient "disposition" or nature. If he has not been patient and reliant,

d. *What other occasion for patience will I have?*

that heals the illness of aversion? "What other means will I have as an occasion for patience?" The sense is "none."

Now, to show that defilement has come to mean subservience, he says:

23. *Held by demonic defilement, their minds are agitated;*
Feverish, they cannot even try to help themselves;
As I observe the world, worthy of my regard,
O Chieftain, aversion is born, but nothing of compassion.

Invoking "the Chieftain," he shows that in his own mind no compassion at all is born, but only aversion.

For whom is compassion not born? For "the world." What is it [the world] like? "Consumed by demonic defilement, their minds are agitated." The defilements—desire-attachment, aversion and so forth—being fearful and oppressive, are like demons (rākṣasa). Held and controlled by them, the mental continuum has been enslaved. Hence it is "feverish." Their minds have problems; they have become drunk with negative directions. For that reason they have entirely neglected the means for working for their own welfare; they do not even try to take the initiative in activities that would relieve their sufferings in this world and the next.

Alternatively, because they are agitated by the defilements, those of the world do themselves harm: They leap into the abyss, they prepare poison to eat.[54]

They are "worthy of regard": Observing any one of them a thought of pity should be born; he should be an object of compassion, for he is an occasion for coming into accord with the course of the bodhisattva. Thus they are relevant to one's regard. But when he sees them to be like that, because of the great power of the defilements, only aversion is born and not compassion.

Now, to show the way in which one comes under the sway of defilement even while abiding in the way proper to oneself, he says:

24abc. *People course in the fruits of their own activity,*
Aware of the inevitable dissolution of all;
Having even examined the blamelessness of others,

"People" refers to worldlings, created by previous activity (karma) and defilement. They "course in the fruits of their own activity." That is to say, they are coursing in the agreeable and disagreeable ripened fruits of whatever activities they have performed, each with his own body, speech and mind. Because of which, although they experience suffering that proceeds from external conditions, these are the fruits of their own past course of action and so not the fault of others. Furthermore, all sentient beings are aware not only of their own inevitable dissolution, but also that everything, because it possesses a momentary character, is impermanent. Hence one's own experience of pleasure and suffering has proceeded from oneself:[55] it can be considered no fault of others.

Although they may have intellectually examined and come to know that it is his or her own problem, they are unable to acquiesce in it. Their own minds being bewildered and obscured by the darkness of ignorance, they are capable rather of deceptive projection out of the fog of unawareness.[56] This being a great wonder, he exclaims:

d. *See their projections out of foggy confusion!*

And to illustrate that miracle, he says:

25ab. *I myself, though an ocean of faults,*
Do not tolerate even a fraction of someone [else]'s;

"Among them I myself am doubtless possessed of demeaning faults of the body-mind continuum—desire-attachment and the other defilements—and of the unwholesome activities that proceed from them, as many and vast as [the waters of] the sea. That I nonetheless do not tolerate—cannot bear—even so much as a drop or a fraction of the most subtle sort of fault in someone else, my mind is indeed a great wonder!"

Furthermore,

c. *I count patience a blessed quality in another,*[57]

"Patience" here indicates not only that which functions as the antidote to anger; it also possesses boundless blessed qualities that result in physical beauty and so forth.[58]

Alternatively, one might gloss this line: "The blessed quality of another's patience," that is to say, the blessed qualities of constancy in patience and in morality, on the part of others who possess these qualities.

d. *But for this I am not patient—here's the wonder!*

For which reason, "Although the qualities of patience may be boundless, I cannot adhere to, nor be constant in even a fraction of them. This is the wonder of my mind, with its essential nature of delusion." The sense is that "it is astonishing."

"But" shows that this appears to be a contradiction. For there is a contradiction in being an ocean of faults, yet intolerant of fault and in the boundless qualities [of patience], yet not adhering to them.

To show how those faults arise, he says:

26. *As though rising into the springtime sky,*
Masses of cloud defilements in my mind
Come and go again and again;
Unabashed, I am wretchedly apathetic.

As in the season of spring, masses of rainclouds gather and rise in the sky and then rain falls, so in the sky of his mind suddenly[59] arise masses of defilements—desire-attachment and so forth. Because they resemble clouds, they are cloudlike masses; many of them arise. They arise in what way? The sense is that "they come and go again and again."

Constantly, again and again, at random they go and return. Just as clouds arise and wander in the sky, letting fall streams of rain, so the defilements are always emerging or arising in his mind, germinating a rain of misdeeds and then letting it fall.

Because of them, he has alienated the mental factor of self-conscious shame at the possession and process of such defilement. Hence to have not resorted to vigor to eliminate the defilements, to have come under the sway of apathy, "is most wretched and censurable of me."

Now he shows that he has grown out of harmony with concentration (samādhi), the means to dispel defilement:

27ab. *But even if the cold wind of defilement has come to arise*
And been zealously defeated with a blaze of concentration,

"Defilement" refers to desire-attachment and the rest. It is like a severe cold wind, in that it defiles the body and mind, becoming the excuse for harmful things such as breaking moral discipline.[60] As the body, when numbed by a cold wind, is incapable of effort, so when hardpressed by the chill of defilement, one cannot proceed on the noble path; thus it is like cold. When it has "come to arise," with ignorance as cause and must be dispelled from the mental continuum, by what is it dispelled? By making the mind one-pointed from development of the antidote: "concentration."

How in particular? "Defeat with a blaze . . . ." From the friction stick of meditation arises the blazing fire of mystic intuition (jñāna), which will outshine and defeat the cold wind of defilement, because of which it resembles fire, the antidote to cold.

Working in this way energy and effort have resulted, "But . . . ."

What fault ensues when thus exerting oneself?

cd. *With the spreading smoke of drowsiness and languor,*
Desires for a bed proceed to grow.

"Drowsiness": entered by which, thought is collected in subservience. "Languor": by which the mind is stunned and unable to grasp its object very well. These two, being causes of ignorance, are termed "smoke." Their "spread" is the capability to overshadow mental clarity by proceeding with a fierce impact.

For that reason, "desires for a bed proceed to grow." With the impact of drowsiness and languor, he cannot focus on the object of concentration and there proceed thoughts that desire by any means to lie in a comfortable bed. [In short], laziness comes to spread.

Since he cannot resort to the antidote to the defilements, what ensues?

28a. *My mind is rendered helpless by the noose of desire-attachment,*

"My mind, devoid of concentration, has come under the sway of defilement and so is rendered helpless by the noose of desire-attachment."

"Desire-attachment" indicates clinging and attachment to sense objects. Because it constitutes a firm bond, it is like a noose. Since the mental continuum is tied subservient to it—rendered helpless to release itself—it is said to be "rendered helpless." "Made powerless" is the sense.

b. *Burned by the fire of aversion, conquered by the conceits;*

Any virtues favorable to the noble path (ārya-mārga) abiding in his continuity have been burned and consumed by the mental fires of enmity.

"Conquered by the conceits": The mental continuity is puffed up by conceit, greater conceit and so forth and robbed of its spiritual (ārya) wealth.[61]

Is it merely the case that these [virtues] are consumed? Not so:

cd. *All filled with weapons, the arrows and the spears*
Of all the faults, I am helplessly stupefied.

Whatever the faults, all of them: "all the faults." Beyond the defilements already mentioned, this includes [all] the others, plus the hosts of subsidiary defilements (upakleśa).

These defilements, inasmuch as they are keen and pierce the mental continuum very subtly, are like "arrows." Piercing in a coarse way, so as to produce critical injury, they are like "spears." Whatever weapons there be of that sort, his mental continuum is "all filled" by them.

Like weapons that leave barbs [inside] and hack up the outside, the defilements constituted by latent tendencies and total ensnarement fill his mind.[62] For that reason he has grown exceedingly discouraged in his helplessness to make effort in the antidote factors and incapable of effort on the noble path. Or, he is "stupefied"—"as though drunk" is the sense.

And to show the other faults of the mind ruled by defilement, he says:

29. *Finding my memory, bound and soon atremble,*
Crushed, I am dissolved;
Lured by pretense and delusion
I circle through the lower range of Māra.

The mind thus overcome by defilement and abiding virtually stupefied recovers its memory,[63] resettling into its original state of composure. But even so he is "bound" by renewed defilements, coming under their sway. He is soon atremble at them. Not remaining long in the mode of mind's original composure, he is crushed in agitation and terror by the weapons of the host of defilements. He is overwhelmed, being dissolved (vilīna) in his inability to make effort toward the object of mental concentration; he is devoid of that capability. With that he comes under the sway of negative thoughts and further defilements such as dishonesty.[64] He has been lured by them and has lost (vilīna) the noble path. Hence his mind is without the power of the antidote [i.e., concentration], its capability feeble (dīna) and low (hīna). He remains under the sway of unawareness, dwelling in the midst of heaps of defilement, "the range of Māra." The sense is that he comes for a long time to wander aimlessly in circles.[65]

To dispel such defilement there is the cultivation of calm (śamatha) and insight (vipaśyanā); but he cannot focus his mind:

30. *Whatever, however I envisage for the calm state,*
Focusing, refocusing the mind there upon it,
From this the noose of defilement
Drags me helpless toward objects with the rope of attachment.

"In whatever manner, whatever [I envisage] for the calm state": He makes a mental image, positioned in the manner of meditating with one-pointedness on the object of visualization. In order to attain that one-pointedness, he focuses the mind over and over there upon it—upon whatever the object of concentration may be—and trains himself in one-pointedness. Nonetheless, he does not so remain. "From this object of visualization":

The firm noose of remaining defilement, attracted toward and settling down upon the five sensual objects, is a "rope" of gazing at [objects] external to mind.[66] In this way the stream of thought is helplessly "dragged" or diverted from its inward focus upon the object of visualization.

This is being shown: Whenever thought has been collected inward by the power of calming meditation in order to dispel the host of differentiations (vikalpa), then, while it is focused on the object without conceptual theorizing (kalpa) and without the natural detachment from dharmas that comes of wisdom,[67] one will come under the sway of previously experienced objects that have been stirred up by the host of defilements, and one will be diverted.

However that may be, may he not, attending to effort fixed on the object, establish an equilibrium (samādhyate)?

31a. *If I tend to diligence, excitedness ensues;*

"Diligence" in this context should be taken as proceeding conscientiously, with energy, in a wholesome direction—not as the persistence that proceeds from an arousal by desire-attachment or aversion, as for example diligence or whatever for the recapture of Sītā and Draupadī as it appears in the *Ramāyana* and *Bharata* epics.

Hence, we have here the antidote to laziness. When relying upon and maintaining his application of vigor, since diligence weakens mental calm, his thoughts emerge excited, stimulated regarding externals.

That being the case, does one reject diligence as well?

bcd. *Relinquishing that, depression is produced;*
Its proper balance being difficult to find,
What shall I do for my agitated mind?

Seeing the fault of becoming excited, he has rejected that diligence, given up the effort. In that case mind becomes inwardly depressed and there is no further focusing upon the visualization.

So we see that although there may be, among the operative

modes of this mind endowed with defilement, a [way of] being without the twin modes of excitement and depression—a state of balancing the pair, or "entering a proper mental balance" (samādhīyate)—it is a thing very difficult to find and attain. So, "My mind being unstable, agitated by the host of defilements, what shall I do?" The sense is that problems will ensue according to both modes; "without that stability, in what shall I course?"

"Since the acceptance-rejection pair comes to realization through wisdom, one should rely upon this."[68] To which he says:

2abc. *Coursing in wisdom, excitedness will emerge:*
Holding to restraint, depression will be born;
Its integration being difficult to find,

"Wisdom" is defined as exact apprehension encompassing the generic and individual characteristics of dharmas. If he comes to course in it otherwise than exactly so, excitedness will emerge; for skipping along thus after the various objects of "mind," he cannot be calm.[69]

If he rejects this and then restrains the mind by way of focusing on whatever be the object of the calming meditation, holding only to inward collectedness, in that case he is deprived of wisdom; in order to withdraw from objects he has eliminated his clear share of wise understanding, and within his mind depression will be born.

So "placing a yoke"[70] to this dis-integration . . . . Keeping a balance of the calm-insight pair is termed "integration" (yuganaddha). As with a balanced yoke (yuga) of oxen one can neatly work even very hard soil, so whenever the calm-insight pair is in a state of balance, like a lamp untroubled by the wind,[71] during that period there is born a mystic intuition that eliminates the host of defilements. In the beginner's mind this marriage is very difficult to find, and it [the mind] is incapable of remaining so. Hence his mind has come under the sway of defilement, and he says:

d. *What shall I do for my agitated mind?*

The sense is that "My mind, devoid of calm and insight, is

incapable of remaining in action. How shall I course in such a state of agitation and wandering? How shall I practice?

"With nothing but effort toward that very aim, certainly one will make progress."

33ab. *Proceeding with perseverance, excitedness will result;*
Relaxing that, depression will be born;

If he sets forth conscientiously with great perseverance to establish his mind in the mode of integration and so forth—if he makes effort—then that mind grows excited and unsettled. Thus defeated, he gains no mental stability from the effort.[72] That being the case, if, in order to reverse it, he relaxes the persevering mind and gives up the effort, then thought grows inwardly depressed and sunken with problems such as forgetting the object of visualization. And while remaining in such a mode there is no growth of a mind one-pointed in concentration.

So he says:

c. *Its middle way being difficult to find,*

For this mind, thus endowed with the faults of excitedness and depression, the "middle way" (madhyama-pratipad)—progressing in the mean, free from both extremes of depression and excitement, a state of balance—is very difficult to find. Because mind is intractable by its very nature, it has only come under the sway of negativity.

So he says:

d. *What shall I do for my agitated mind?*

Although mind is by nature pure and luminous, it has been agitated by a host of adventitious defilements; it has become polluted, and the reflection of the right meaning cannot arise in it and be seen. "How should I abide, how should I proceed?" he confesses, by way of describing the faults of mind itself.

Now, to show that grasping at a "self," which has proceeded from ignorance, is the root of all fault, he says:

34a. *Over and over, with the forest fire of meditation,*

"Meditation" (dhyāna) means establishing an equilibrium; it refers to the four trances (dhyāna) and so forth.[73] By it the thicket of defilement is burned and consumed. So it is like a great fire spreading through the forest. With such fire, "over and over," at each moment . . . .

What does it do?

b. *The jungle of fault may be burned, yet*

The "faults" of desire-attachment and so forth, being many and being a basis for burning, are like a jungle. Although they be burned and dispelled by the fire of meditation, yet

c. *The fixed root of "self" being unconsumed,*

Grasping at "I" and "mine," in that it is the basis for the growth of the defilements, is like a root which, having developed from beginningless time, is very stable; it has neither been burned nor consumed and so is regenerated.

In what manner?

d. *It comes to life in advance, as though moistened by rain.*

In springtime, although the grass and trees have been burned [by the summer sun], any which has not been burned to the root, when it encounters moisture, will be regenerated. The view of self being likewise the root of all faults, if it has not been eliminated, then in association with sensory objects as the causal condition (pratyaya), it is brought to life in the advance of his defiled lifestyle.

Will not only the wisdom portion suffice, seeing as it does the lack of self in personality and dispelling the root of defilement?

35ab. *For some the flux of mere defilement-karma-fruition,*
By being seen, will be diverted;

"Defilement" refers to desire-attachment, aversion and the rest. "Karma" has a wholesome, unwholesome or indeterminate nature. "Fruition" is [its] ripening.

As for "mere": Apart from [that of] the gods, from the Ruler (īśvara) on down, the fruition of defilement and karma is merely limited, whereas aside from it, there is no Creator.[74]

Their "flux" is the process of a stream of moments. Seeing it—seeing with the yogic practice of analysis, wise understanding endowed with mindfulness and full awareness—the view of self is furthermore diverted.[75] For upon a detailed examination, the so-called "self" is not established [to exist] apart from that which proceeds from the flux of saṁsāra—which is nothing but mere karma and defilement.

Not merely diverting it, but,

c. *Do they not eliminate even the flow of thought?*

The noble auditors have examined the reality (bhāva) behind the Truth of Suffering: the flow of thought that abides in a momentary manner, the aggregate of consciousness that is the substrate [of existence]. And by the production, as its antidote, of what they term "emptiness of consciousness"—the Truth of the Path that envisages the Truth of Cessation—have they not eliminated it in accordance with its contrary, its antidote?[76] But the reality of emptiness ensues, and without envisaging oneself and others,

d. *This is quite far from interest in the welfare of the world.*

Because they are devoid of the special wisdom that views [beings] as neither empty nor nonempty at one and the same time, while they remain in saṁsāra they are depressed by suffering and so unable to fulfill the aims of others. Such is the sense.

How are they far from the welfare of the world?

36a. *The guardians part only from attachment,*

"Guardian" refers to guarding one's own continuum with Dharma associated with the four Noble Truths. Or, it may be taken as [the guardians, *tāyin*], those "worthy of offerings," the noble arhats.

They are freed "only from attachment"—only from the craving constituted by affections bound up with saṁsāra. By having rejected that, they are parted from it, and moreover,

b. *Regardless of all the world;*

Whatever the world may be, and however many be all those in all of it, so, "all the world": everyone included within the triple realm.

Having become "regardless" of it: They have come to abandon the effort of caring to participate in extricating [others] from saṁsāra, in liberating them from suffering; they are intent upon their own welfare.

"Their flow of thought is nirvanized." To show this he says:

cd. *The flow of thought, like a lamp whose cause is exhausted,*
Enters nirvāṇa, the remaining aggregates consumed.

Here "thought" is understood to be essentially consciousness. Its "flow" is the entirety of its succession from moment to moment.

When that flow has come to be purified and transmuted in mystic intuition (jñāna), then it is "like a lamp whose cause is exhausted." As when oil, the cause of a lamp, has been consumed, the lamp comes to be without blaze, so the mystic intuition that has proceeded from adamantine concentration eliminates the defilements together with the impressions [that produce them], and they thus enter nirvāṇa.[77] This is moreover the nirvāna "without remainder."[78] The sense is this: The sum total of the remaining aggregates produced by previous karma and defilement are burned, consumed and rendered nonexistent by the fire of gnosis (jñāna). Then [the arhats] come to abide in the sphere of nirvāṇa (nirvāṇa-dhātu). Hence they are quite far from working the welfare of the world.

Granted that such welfare of the world proceeds from the thought of awakening;[79] to show now that it and his own continuum are incompatible, he says (*37*):

37a. *Whatever dispels the distress of all the world—*

"Whatever" refers to the thought of awakening. With what sort of qualities is it endowed? "It dispels the entire distress of the world." It entirely dispels—makes nonexistent—the derangement or distress caused by all the suffering—the three sorts of suffering—of all sentient beings comprised by the four manners of birth who abide [in saṁsāra] up to the peak of existence.[80]

b. *The thought of awakening: ambrosia, elixir—*

"The thought of awakening" having the nature of resolving upon and setting forth for awakening[81]—how is it distinguished? "Ambrosia, elixir." As the ambrosia eater is not struck by death, so the thought of awakening sustains the life of the noble path and occasions the attainment of all its ranks. So it is like ambrosia. Resorting to the medicine "elixir," white hair and wrinkles are dispelled and one is made free from illness; likewise the thought of awakening occasions the defeat of suffering and defilement belonging to one's own continuity and to that of others as well.

Since it possesses such qualities, one must take it to heart; therefore:

c. *When I develop the nonconceptual as cause of awakening,*

"Awakening" (bodhi) refers to mystic intuition constituting the knowledge of all modes.[82] As the cause and basis for attaining it, he "develops nonconceptualization" (akalpanā). By means of eliminating perceived and perceiver, he trains his attention upon the undiffused meaning.[83]

Does mind so remain in that condition? Not so:

d. *Then I am only chasing differentiations.*

While training himself to realize the great intuition (mahājñāna) of the thought of awakening, "then I am only chasing differentiations." Because he is only a beginner, he is chasing what is no more than a differentiation. As to the meaning of "differentiation" (vikalpa): He chases after various clumsy differentiations that have been generated by misrepresentation (saṁkalpa). The sense is that he is sidetracked.[84]

The term "only" (eva) indicates independence of other modes; it shows that there is no other object. So the basis of his thought is reliance upon differentiation only; there is no other. As for example in the line: "Only Arjuna wields the bow; there is none beside."[85]

To this it may be objected, "This is not correct. It has been explained that:

The rivers, the oceans, the mountains—
These are transformations of thought.[86]

Since nothing exists aside from thought, is it not inappropriate to designate 'support' and 'supported'?"[87] That may be so. But in the Sautrāntika method,[88] there is no contradiction in defining both thought and object as established.

Continuing to develop, however, there are other ways that enable him to dispel differentiation:[89]

38a. *All the world is like a dream . . .*

"[Like] a dream" because it is apt to appear even though it be unfamiliar from one's previous experience—that is to say, deceptive.[90]

In the case of a dream, even without an object of attachment such as a popular beauty (janapada-kalyāṇī), or an object of antagonism and hatred, there is the appearance.

"Like" means "corresponding with that." What is it that corresponds? "The world": things found in this hollow state of saṁsāra.

How does it correspond?

—by no one
b. *Is there any act of perception whatsoever;*

In line with this, there is no act of perception or grasping whatsoever at any things, be they subtle or coarse, that we call "objects" or "perceptibles," by any differentiator or perceiver among those of the world.

For example: In a dream one may behold objective things in various pleasant and unpleasant modes, and they may also function as objects upon which to settle down. But because they are an error by their very nature they have, rightly speaking, no existence whatsoever.

cd. *Even having cultivated, I course in the very range*
Of the enemy: differentiation of conceiver and conceived.

Not only has he heard and become aware that "All dharmas are like a dream," he has over and over cultivated and exercised the meaning. Nonetheless—as is the sense of "even"—"I have come under the sway of differentiation."

And what is that differentiation like? "Conceiver and . . . ." When formulating a conception, there must be a conceiver—a mind that does the grasping (cittaṁ grāhakam). When discovering and penetrating, there must be something to be conceived—objects to be grasped (viṣayāṇi grāhyāṇi). In the existence of these two is the particular conceptualization—a differentiation of conceiver and conceived. The sense is "differentiation of objective and subjective" (grāhya-grāhaka-vikalpa).

That [process] is itself a direction adverse to selflessness and nondiscrimination, so, "the enemy." The sense is this: The range (spyod-yul, gocara) of such a nemesis as differentiation is that "I am always coursing (spyod, caramāṇa) in objectification (yul-du gyur-pa-nyid, viṣaya-varttitā); I have come under its influence." Or, one may say, "I have been defeated by it: Aware that they are fraudulent as a dream, I have withdrawn the mind from objects and put an end to development. But then I come to be defeated by the hosts of defilement [that have developed in my mind] from beginningless ages of time."

Having thus become aware of the difficulty of turning away differentiation, and the impotence of his own antidotes, he demonstrates request of the Lord himself:

39ab. *O Chieftain, this quite unendurable hurt—*
Observe it and grant me the immaculate view;

"Chieftain" is an invocation. He is "chieftain" as the lord of all dharmas,[91] or as the healer of all defilement diseases.

"This quite unendurable hurt" refers to harm proceeding from the current of defilement—desire-attachment and so forth—within his own mental continuum, causing immediate and continuing affliction of the mental-physical continuum that is fierce and very hard to bear and which has become evident. "See this and grant me the immaculate view": Pray grant the right view, the medicine for these injuries, which is unsoiled by stains of faults incompatible with it.

But have these [injuries] not been produced by virtue of his own efforts?

cd. *Whatever I cherish, whatever preoccupies me,*
Those very things frustrate me at the start.

The immeasurable things that may be thus cherished and prized . . . . Or, a particular antidote path congenial with the perfections . . . . While discursively preoccupied with whatever that path may be, "it becomes at first only [a source of] frustration and anxiety." In short, the sense is that: "Whatever antidote I may rely upon to defeat the host of defilements is, by reason of its impotence, overwhelmed by negative alternatives."

To show now that "these problems are my own fault," he says:

40ab. *But what can the Lord do for faults*
That I myself have created before?

To this "but" is to be added: "Since the faults come from myself, what effect can someone [else] have?"

When was the creation of these faults? "Created before": in previous lifetimes that have succeeded one another from time immemorial, because they have been generated by misrepresentation, and because of their accumulation as distorted impressions.[92]

What is the point? "My faults are like this: Even having sought to rely upon and to prize the antidote, [there remains] this deepseated problem of faults such as being under the sway of falsity (mithyatva)."

"The Lord" is conqueror of the four māras, ["the Lord" because he] possesses the six qualities of the Ruler and other [gods].[93] The Buddha is at issue.

In such a case, O Lord, "What can you do?"; it is hard to treat. To have come under the sway of defilement and to wander in circles on the range of Māra is one's own fault. Since worldlings are responsible for their own actions,[94] they course in the fruition of karma created by themselves; the creator of pleasure and suffering is not the Lord. That is why he has declared in the scripture: "I am the field, but I am not the seed."

To illustrate that very point with a simile, he says:

c. *The dispeller of darkness for all the world, the very sun*

Because it is a matter of everything in the whole world, he says "all the world." And because it illumines everything in the same way, "world" should be taken to refer to the animate and inanimate both.

Their "darkness" is gloom without light. What dispels and defeats it? This [line] is answer to that.

Who is it? "The sun": the thousand-rayed.

The very sun, possessor of such qualities,

d. *Cannot dispel the black darkness of those who have been born blind.*

Although it cannot indeed dispel and defeat the black darkness of those blind from the moment of birth, that is not the fault of the sun, but has proceeded from a fault of the blind themselves.

Likewise the Buddha, the Lord, the Sun of Dharma, courses with the rays of good Dharma, as contained in the three collections, to conquer the darkness of unawareness abiding in the hearts of the world. Even so, the failure to dispel the faults of those who, settling down in wrong views, are devoid of the wisdom eye is the fault of the world itself, not that of the Teacher.

Having thus spoken to the essential nature of his faults, to show how it is furthermore difficult to be healed by the noble path, he says:

41. *Relying for so long upon what is unhealthy*
And having constant mental infatuation with it,
I am punished with leprous hands and feet;
What can I do by occasional reliance on medicine?

"As medicine at the end is not a suitable treatment for the disease of leprosy, what can I do?" should be added.

Why is he leprous? "Relying for so long upon what is unhealthy." Whatever activity occasions the germination of leprosy—unhealthiness such as improper food and path of action[95]—relying upon that and maintaining it for a long time is "unhealthy." Beyond that is the continual or "constant mental infatuation" [with that activity]. He cannot maintain, even occasionally, the application of means for dispelling it. ("And" indicates that not only does he rely upon what is unhealthy, he also longs for it in his heart.)

How again? "Punished with leprous hands and feet." Through the influence of abiding in such unhealthiness and through a lack of medical attention, the whole body is suffused with leprosy. At last even the hands and feet are punished, becoming rotten.[96] Even if the leper should, for the space of some moments, rely upon—that is to say, take—an antileprosy medicine, it does not provide a healing benefit. So "What can I do?" The sense is that "I will not become free of disease by that [means]."[97]

The implication is that, because the current of defilement included within his own continuum is in fact the view of self, he has held and even clung to that view for a long space of time and failed to seek its antidote, the noble path. All of this constitutes the unsuitable treatment: He has not done what should be done by means of the right path.

And to show another simile for his growth in a faulty manner, he says:

42a. *The tree of thought, from beginningless ages of time,*

"Thought" is the entirety of consciousness. Because it resembles a tree, he cites the tree as example.

For how long has it grown? "From beginningless ages of time." Time is that which has no beginning, so "beginningless ages ot time." "Ages of time" refers to its delimitation by sun, moon, planets, stars and so forth, and this term also indicates that there is no beginning either to saṁsāra.[98]

During such time, by what does the tree grow?

b. *Moistened and fostered by the bitter sap of defilement,*

"Defilement" refers to desire-attachment and the rest. They are ignoble and, being poisonous and unsavory to the taste, are a "bitter sap." Like the sap of the Nimba and other [trees with bitter fruit], it grows and spreads moistened by sap of that sort. For that reason,

c. *I cannot make a sweet tasting substance of it;*[99]

The sense is that just as trees with that bitter taste, moistened and grown with water that is bitter also, cannot fashion [fruit] whose nature is sweet and so forth, so also the nature of thought that has grown up with defilement is hard to transform by means of the noble path.

With how much?

d. *What will it become with a drop of quality water?*

What will come of pouring one drop of water endowed with the eight good qualities—sweetness and so forth—on such a tree as that? All will not become delicious.

Likewise, the sense is this: There are difficulties in transforming or treating, by means of the right path, the essential nature of thought that has grown up with the defilements from beginningless ages of time. One will not purge the host of defilements, nor will the dharmas of the noble path come to grow with only a drop of the quality water of antidote factors.

To show once more the faults of the mental gateway, he says:[100]

43a. *My mind has all the faults by its very nature;*

"Because of the agitation caused by the host of defilements in my mind, I am devoid of deliberation as to what should be rejected and accepted. This, and the faults that result in harm to others—desire-attachment, aversion and the rest—abide in my essential nature, in my very being." And since the thought of awakening is the best antidote for dispelling fault, he says:

bcd. *Great wonder should awakening become the philosopher's stone!*
Even as I apply myself to just that quality,
I continue to be the very substance of fault.

"Awakening" is the supreme intuition (anuttara-jñāna). However, in regard to the mind that will attain it, "awakening" is referred to in the manner of designating the cause by its effect; it is like a potion that transmutes [things] into gold. Just as iron is changed into gold by [the process] known as "quicksilver reappearing as gold with the philosopher's stone," so the thought of awakening refines the mind of its saṁsāric defilements, transmuting it into right intuition; hence it resembles the philosopher's stone.[101] "All-knowing mystic intuition" (sarvajña-jñāna) is the sense.

For the same reason, it would be a "great wonder," astonishing. By an initial application to just that fact of awakening's possession of many sorts of abundant qualities, by the generation of the intention [to attain it][102] and so forth, he has begun[103] to refine the mental continuum. But because he has not followed up on it, "I continue to be the very substance of fault." Even having applied himself to the thought of awakening adorned with both mundane and supramundane qualities,[104] he comes under the sway of defilement. Accepting that which acts as the very substance—the essential nature—of physical, verbal and mental faults, and holding tightly to it, thus he continues. The implication is that [his mind] cannot hold onto good qualities any more than can the mind of a drunkard; rather, he has become, and causes himself to remain, a wellspring of fault.

The sense might be summarized thus: Just as unprepared iron and the like, although it may be anointed with philosopher's stone, will not give up its substance, so this unprepared mind as well, even when applied to the qualities of the thought of awakening, does not give up its problems of fault.

Now to show the relevance of that gold-transmuting awakening, he says:

44a. *Whatever is taught as the great medicine itself,*

Inasmuch as it heals the disease of defilement, it is "the great medicine": whatever has been taught or demonstrated which functions as a path, an antidote, a Dharma gateway, beginning with "love." Whatever path may have been taught him, as for example the unclean as antidote to desire-attachment, love as antidote to aversion, or dependent origination as antidote to bewilderment . . .

b. *Just that becomes poison for me;*

"Although there may be no other [relevant teaching], just that holy medicine in particular, because I myself in particular have such wretched fortune as to have come under the sway of defilement, becomes poison for me. Just as one may die or be made ill to the point of death, by reason of a faulty application and so forth of medicine, so for me this medicine of Dharma becomes distorted; because it produces defilement, it 'becomes poison.'"

In such a state as that, by what may one be healed?

c. *Were there a better elixir which were relevancy itself,*

"Relevancy" would be mind seeking a relevant path or resting assured in meditation and concentration or eliminating defilement through progress by faith and investigation by wisdom. This relevance is taught to consist of reliance upon the good Dharma as declared by the Lord.

This is "a better elixir." Following the declaration of the Teacher—taking it to heart—is the cause of dispelling the disease of defilement and of freedom from the suffering of saṁsāra; so it is distinguished from profane (prākṛta) elixir; it is "better." Were there such, how could it be obtained?

d. *If I have no confidence, it does not truly exist.*

The sense is that beyond this [possible existence of a better elixir], if he has come under the sway of defilement and so has not an absolute faith in the path and, without that certainty, lacks confidence [in it], then that relevance has no real existence. From proceeding with absolute faith toward the realization of buddhahood, one comes to be released (mukta). If one has absolute faith, the intention of awakening is generated, and it is inherently logical to come from that gradually to release.[105]

"Confidence," however, must be taken as "happiness": the pleasure and mental ease of one-pointed mental concentration born of equilibrium. If that [above-mentioned] relevance capable of eliminating defilement does exist, but one is without happiness and the mind is unsettled, [true] relevance does not exist and there ensues defeat by the defilements.[106]

To show now just what that relevance is, he says: "Certain defilements" and so forth. Here "relevant" means eliminating defilement, so,

5abc. *Whatever dispels certain more intense defilements*
And does not cause the production of others,
That is called "relevant"; being in my mind . . .

In possessing that which may be relevant he eliminates, with their antidotes, the defilements such as desire-attachment, aversion and bewilderment that have grown intense, that have grown into a style of life. This is not the highest means, as has been shown above. So [he engages in] right preoccupation, a calmed version of sordid discursive preoccupation, as antidote to the cause of suffering. By having exercised the noble path of meditation instructions with attentive devotion to the path of application, before long, by discerning the principle (tattva) in that host of defilements, they are tranquilized.[107] There remain however certain faults, among the host of defilements, that remain in motion. Among them, some reside in the mental continuum in the form of latent tendencies; others are incidental faults. The path of antidotes that does not produce troubling and disturbing [incidental faults], as for example aversion when developing the repulsive as antidote to desire-attachment, he calls "relevant." It is being consistent with authoritative standards of knowledge (pramāṇa) and associated with logical formulation (hetu) that generates right intuition; such a thing is termed "relevant·"

"Although I may be aware of it in my mind, and indeed know it intellectually, nonetheless . . ."

d. *How then has it not been made certain as well?*

By developing the path[108] of that relevancy which functions as the cause of deliverance (vimukti), one actualizes it (sākṣāt-karoti), upon which the attainment of gnosis is "certified." Because he has not attained that, he says: "How then has it not been made certain as well?" [The answer is that] "I have not exercised that relevant path." He is showing that "Although I may have made it known by the wisdom that comes of having heard and contemplated the right path as promulgated by the Teacher, it has not been actualized with the wisdom of meditative development."[109]

Having shown the fruits of the thought of awakening, now he shows the fruits of development:

46abc. *The impressions of predisposition, tendency and element—*
Applying myself to the antidote for [these] causes of fault—
When I develop the instructions for meditation,

"Predisposition" (āśaya) refers to intention (adhyāśaya); it is a matter of attitude.[110] "Tendencies" (anuśaya) are the subtle extensions of desire-attachment and so forth.[111] "Element" (dhātu) means nature (svabhāva).[112]

"Impressions" (vāsanā) are those very predispositions and so forth, as impressions abiding in the mind. They refer to whatever the mind possesses in the way of faults that have resulted from the impressions of predisposition, tendency and element. With these [impressions, there is] the cause for coming to birth of desire-attachment, aversion and so forth. Whatever the [causes] may be—the view of self and so forth—he applies the mind to their antidote—to directions adverse to them—as for example to selflessness or to the unclean; he fixes his mind to it. Beyond that, in order to actualize those meditation instructions that have already been made certain by the wisdom of hearing and contemplating the sense of what the Teacher has (1) declared, in distinct vehicles, after considering the gradations of superior, middling and inferior faculties, or (2) declared to be the various antidotes to desire-attachment, aversion and bewilderment; by developing and exercising that, he has formed one-pointedness, and from that the host of defilements becomes calm.

They become so in how much time?

d. *Here, before long, they grow calm.*

In this condition, because he has well developed—put his mind to—this method of instruction, before long—soon—the host of defilements belonging to his mind is dispelled; it grows calm. The sense is that the defilements of those who make progress by continuing to develop themselves correctly are not difficult to eliminate.

Now, to show those same declarations of the Lord to be honesty itself, he says:

47a. *O Guardian, completely devoid of all faults,*

"Guardian": Because he guards living beings from suffering, he is the "guardian." "Faults" are dharmas of those in saṁsāra, desire-attachment and the rest. He is devoid of them all; they are eliminated.

Again, what is he like?

b. *Who sees the highest meaning of all dharmas,*

Whatever dharmas there be, all of them—so, "all dharmas": those with outflows and those without, animate and inanimate, near and far. The "highest meaning" of these dharmas is the extraordinary meaning. Because he possesses the character of discerning it, he is called the one "who sees the highest meaning of all dharmas."

c. *By expounding it in various modes as well,*

Because there are various modes of faculty and inclination, he makes his declarations breaking it down into several modes of vehicle. Or, because there are boundless modes of defilement, there are modes of antidote as well, and [this line may be taken to indicate] their various declarations. These eliminate the entire host of defilements—desire-attachment and the rest—together with the impressions [that give rise to them]:

d. *You entirely dispel the seeds of defilement.*

The sense is that "You entirely dispel all defilements of the triple realm."

Having thus explained the qualities of his teaching, now to show how to eliminate the defilements by seeing his physical form and hearing his voice, it is said (*48*):

48ab *Your body blazing with marks of beauty,*
As I see the presence before me,

O Lord, whatever be the beauties of your physical form (rūpakāya), those are its marks, so, "marks of beauty." It is marked by the thirty-two signs, beginning with possession of the topknot, and the eighty proportions.[113] Hence he is blazing in a cascade of shining enlightenment; his complexion is greatly blazing like the gold of Jambu River.[114]

"As [I see] the presence of such a body before me" means that he has come to see it directly before the faculty [of sight], or that he sees it intellectually, making it evident as though actually present before the mind. And furthermore,

c. *So I come to hear the nectar drunk by ear;*

Because human beings are to drink it with their two ears, [he says] "drunk by ear." "Perceived by ear" is the sense.

To what is he referring? "So I come to hear the nectar . . . ." "So" is a connective. "O Protector, not only does your form—whether seen directly or mentally visualized as actually present—dispel the defilements, but your voice as well becomes nectar for any human beings who come to hear it." Just as those who drink nectar with their cupped hands come not to be struck by death, so those who adopt the manner of drinking in the nectar of the Protector's voice with the "cupped hands" of their two ears are not struck by the poison of defilement; hence there is no break in the faculty of their life of virtue, and they go to no lower state of rebirth.[115]

d. *The seeds of defilement are entirely destroyed.*

The defilements of human beings who behold such a form and hear such speech, together with the seeds that have caused the germination of suffering through repeated rebirths (saṁsārayati) in the triple realm, are entirely and universally destroyed. The sense is that they wither away and exhaust themselves.

Having thus explained the virtues of seeing the physical form, now to show the virtues of beholding the Dharmabody (dharmakāya), he says (*49*:)

49a. *O Chieftain, you are far superior to that,*

"Chieftain" is a vocative. "You ar far superior to that": One might add that he also possesses a body that is more eminent than the physical form, extraordinary in that it functions as the most superior.

Just what is it?

b. *Possessing also the supreme sun of the Dharmabody;*

By the term "Dharma" he describes the Lord to be extremely subtle, for he is the very reality of Dharma and shows how he is indemonstrable, for he has come into the range of a unique knowledge of everything beyond appearances.[116]

That is his body. "Whatever be the Dharma, that is his body," thus the compound as from "body that is Dharma."[117]

It is like the sun, so, a "sun of the Dharma." For just as the sun dispels the host of outer darkness, so the illumination of the "sphere of Dharma" intuition conquers the blackest darkness, the darkness of ignorance. So it resembles the sun.[118]

Therefore it is "the supreme," for there is nothing beyond it, or because it is not shared by any of those of the stages below.[119]

Hence,

c. *Even with meditation, it eludes the range of the world—*

Although the reality (bhāva) of the Dharmabody may be contemplated and meditatively developed, it comes not into the cognitive range (viṣaya) of creatures of the world of the triple realm, ordinary persons who cling to things. For its essential nature is not to be discovered (adhigama) and penetrated (avabodha) by the intellect.

How then does he know it to exist?

d. *That it conquers the fog of fault: What a great wonder!*

For all that, to conquer and dispel faults that act as a basis for defilement, the fog of black darkness known as "ignorance," which is precisely what the Dharmabody does—being the intuition of emptiness (śūnyatā-jñāna)—it is not envisioned as a thing (vastu); it eludes the range of the eye; yet it occasions the dispelling of the intellectual darkness of human beings—what a great wonder! Being an inconceivable object (acintya-viṣaya), [the Dharmabody] is marvelous!

To demonstrate salutation, describing the Lord's way of good qualities by way of concluding the confession and praise undertaking, he says:

50a. *With whatever high mind is appropriate,*

"Lord, I make salutation, bowing to you" is to be added.

Why make salutation? In order that he may pacify the faults. How? "With whatever high mind is appropriate." Whatever the highest of thoughts, causing the mind to reach beyond the object of the auditors, independent Buddhas and [other ordinary persons] to nondual mystic intuition, that is appropriate.[120]

Envisaging what?

b. *Abiding in whatever calm state is appropriate,*

To the one who, advancing to the heights of trance—along with either the effortless marriage (anābhoga-yuganaddha) of calm and insight or the adamantine concentration—abides in attainment of the perfect conclusion to yoga, I prostrate.

For what purpose?

cd. *Who pacifies all the faults in all the modes,*
Whatever the Lord may be, that I salute.

Whatever the faults that have generated the suffering of saṁsāra, the one who courses to pacify or dispel them all is you yourself. "To repel them" is the sense.

How? "All modes": to dispel "all the modes" bound up with the impressions. Or, to pacify by means of "all modes," to pacify with the various styles of vehicle or with the varieties of means (upāya) such as wonderworking powers and miracles.[121]

Hence, "Whatever the Lord most suitably may be, that I salute." The sense is that "Whatever the Lord who thus pacifies the host of defilements may be, to that I salute and bow with serene reverence of body, speech and mind." He says, "Whatever he be, to that . . . ." for this reason: "Whereas one may discourse in terms that fail to encompass your knowledge, to speak in that way of the Chieftain fails to be relevant." The sense is that "To you, endowed with such qualities, whatever you may be, I prostrate; I take refuge."

Now, to dedicate to sentient beings whatever merit may have proceeded from the composition of this praise—[such] being the code of the bodhisattva, he must accord with it—he says (51):

51a. Such confession to the supremely qualified one,

"Such" indicates the completion. "Supremely qualified": to the one who possesses an extraordinary mass of good qualities, to the Teacher . . . ."Confession" to him: Describing, in his presence, whatever misdeeds and faults he himself has committed.

What has he made by way of [doing] so?

b. By the virtue of framing a proper praise,

By way of describing his own faults he has elaborated or well framed terms of proper praise of the Conqueror. From that, virtue (śubha) or merit (puṇya) is created.

What is it like?

c. Whatever I have gathered, bright like the beautiful moon,

That merit moreover is bright and beautiful as the autumn moon, unpolluted by the smog of fault, agreeable.[122]

"Whatever I have gathered": that which has been accomplished and amassed by myself.

By mentioning the moon (candra) he shows also "My own name is Candra." And by saying "bright," he shows that "My own nature has been purified."

To what does he dedicate that merit?

d. May everyone go to the Land of Bliss.

"By the merit thus gathered by me, may all these living creatures go to the Blissful (sukhāvatī) realm of the world; may they be reborn there.

Alternatively, the supreme bliss (sukha) is the rank of Buddha (sugata). So the sense may be taken as "May they come to attain that [bliss]ful state."

Adhering to the request
Of the great intellect Sumati,
I, Buddhaśānti, composed
This Praise in Confession *comment.*

The vast sphere of Candra's literary topics,
Adhering to the Sugata's profound course,
Done in the mode of praising after confession,
Aims at refining one's existence.

May its commentary, like rays of the moon,
So agreeable for me to compose,
Purge the defilements of the world;
May all attain flawless Buddhahood.

Notes to the Commentary

1. The first sentence introduces verse one, lines a and b (1ab), the second sentence introduces lines c and d (1cd). The Buddha's "causes" are the two accumulations (merit, puṇya; and gnosis, jñāna) and the path to buddhahood. His "effect" is the stage of buddhahood with all its qualities. His "fulfillment of purpose" is turning the wheel of doctrine and leading all living beings to awakening. (Oral communication by Geshe Ngawang Dhargyey, Dharamsala, 1976.)

2. The three basic defilements are mentioned two paragraphs further on: the most basic is "bewilderment" (moha) or ignorance. Numerous subsidiary defilements (upakleśa) that flow from them are mentioned in the course of the text.

3. "Rudra" is an epithet of Śiva. "Technique" (upāya) is otherwise translated "(skill in) means."

4. The "triple realm" (tridhātu) comprises the whole universe: the realm of sense desires (kāma-dhātu), form (rūpa-dhātu) and formlessness (arūpadhātu).

5. "Auditors" (śrāvaka): because they listen to the Dharma (śṛvanti) and cause others to hear (śrāvayanti). This definition from the *Sgra-sbyor-bam-po-gnyis-pa* (abbrev. *Sgra*) in Sonam Angdu, ed., *Tibeto-Sanskrit Lexicographical Materials* (Leh: Basgo Tongspon, 1973). "Independent buddhas" (pratyekabuddha) are also Hīnayāna; they attain liberation independently, without the aid of a buddha in their last lifetime and they may also make the doctrine known to those who request it.

6. "Stream of thought" (cittasaṁtati): the individual, defined without reference to a "self" (pudgala, ātman), as a stream of consciousness composed of discrete moments of awareness.

On "impressions" (vāsanā) see verse 46a and n. 111 below. In the Sautrāntika-Yogācāra theory of karmic causation, actions implant seeds (bīja, see 48d) in the mental continuum (or in the āśraya of the Yogācārins), which create a disposition for future activity—a habit. So the Buddha has eliminated faults and he has eliminated their causes as well, thus removing all the obstacles to gnosis. (But at 36cd the arhats, perfected auditors, are described as having done the same, and the Buddha is implicitly distinguished as working the welfare of the world.)

7. The "qualities" that are "refined" or trained in by the Buddha are the twelve ascetic qualities, MHV no. 1127f. (*Mahāvyutpatti*, ed. Sakaki, repr. Tokyo: Suzuki, 1962). The ten powers (bala) are listed MHV 119f., the four grounds of courage (vaiśāradya) at 130f.

8. "Direct cognition" (pratyakṣa): direct nonconceptual cognition by the mind's eye.

9. "Wind" (vāyu) is a medical term for an overbalance of that humor.

10. "Knowing the path" (mārga-jñatā): the means to buddhahood, based upon bodhicitta and determined to remain in saṁsāra for the benefit of all. See D. S. Ruegg, *La Théorie du Tathāgatagarbha et du Gotra* (Paris: École Française D'Extrême-Orient, 1969. Abbrev. R), pp. 189-205, 218-219.

11. "Ocean" is *chu-bo* (nadī, ogha), also "river" (the ocean being conceived as a salt river surrounding the continents). This verse is reminiscent of the story related by Tāranātha and other historians of Candragomin's ocean crossings. See *Tibet Journal* 7.3 (1982), pp. 10, 18.

12. On *vitarka-vicāra* see Conze, *Buddhist Thought in India* (repr. Ann Arbor: U. Michigan Press, 1967), p. 191. These represent (1) mind's search for the object and application to it and (2) the subsequent investigation of it. Their elimination constitutes calm, śamatha. The commentary glosses them only by their verbal forms.

13. The plural suffix indicated here does not appear in the Tibetan translation of the line.

14. *Lavaṇa-nadī* is the reconstruction of *lan-tshwa'i chu-bo*. The *Saddharma-smṛtyupasthāna* makes reference to a *lan-tshwa zhes-bya-ba'i rgya-mtsho*. (P Mdo Lu 247b.2, O v. 38, p. 267). See also MHV 4166.

Seven "spiritual treasures" are listed at MHV 1565f.: faith, morality, conscience, consideration, learning, renunciation and wisdom.

15. Kāma-rāga and bhāva-rāga. In an older classification of desires, the latter appears as bhava-rāga (MHV 2133): hence, "desire for sensual pleasure and desire for renewed existence." The reading found in this text is corroborated, however, by Guṇaprabha, O 5546, Yi 235a.6-7: desire for sexual intercourse and desire for other things.

16. "Watercourse" (jalāgamā) is the name of a river. See Edgerton (abbrev. E), *Buddhist Hybrid Sanskrit Dictionary* (repr. Delhi: Motilal, 1970), s.v.

17. Variant: "If, to dispel [desires]." "Develops" (bhāvanā): meditative cultivation of an object, lit. "bringing into being." "Vessel" refers to the body. Meditations on the "repulsive" (aśubha) develop the body, for example (*Saundarananda* 17.36): "Then seeing the body to be but an impure aggregate of skin, sinew, fat, blood, bone, flesh, hair, etc. and reflecting on its substance, he did not perceive even the minutest [real substance] in it." At the extreme are meditations on corpses in various stages of decay; see Buddhaghosa, *Visuddhimagga* (abbrev. M), ch. 9 (tr. Bhikkhu Ñāṇamoli, *The Path of Purification* [Kandy: Buddhist Publication Society, 1975]).

18. The causative form is not used in the commentary as it has been in the verse. Perhaps *bya* has degenerated into *ba.*

19. Thus the Buddhist definition of love (maitrī): whether passionate or dispassionate, it desires the welfare of the other. Love is developed in the "four stations of brahma": love, compassion (karuṇā), gladness (muditā) and evenmindedness (upekṣā). The discussion here resembles that of the VM, in which Buddhaghosa reviews the dangers of each station. On love, for example, VM says (in paraphrase): Love promotes the aspect of happiness; it is manifested as the removal of enmity. It succeeds when it makes aversion subside and fails when it produces [selfish] affection. Love has desire-attachment as its near enemy [able to corrupt it by similarity], since both share in seeing good qualities in the object (9.93, 98).

20. "Approval and resentment" (anunaya, pratigha) are the equivalents used by the translator of the VM. Buddhaghosa interprets evenmindedness as a king of moral neutrality, whose near enemy is the tendency to a placid homelife ignoring the faults and virtues of others (9.96, 101). But here its close danger is the opposite: aloofness from the world with disregard of others and lack of compassion. Further on (v. 36), Candragomin implies that equanimity is the final stage of a Hīnayāna path; he accuses the arhat of seeking freedom only from the limited craving that is concern for others.

21. On the "aspects of suffering" as a meditation topic see VM 16.32-60. "Effort" (vyāyāma) is the sixth limb of the noble eightfold path (MHV 1002).

22. "Conceit" (māna) is the first of seven types of pride (MHV 1946-1952): it is regarding oneself as superior to another. "Excessive conceit" (adhimāna) is pride in one's possessions. So this latter type conquers his "wealth" of virtue. Self-pity would come under self-deprecating conceit (ūna-māna).

23. "Mutual emptiness" (itaretara-śūnyatā), which is implied here, is regarded by the *Laṅkāvatāra* as the lowest of seven sorts of emptiness (P Mdo Ngu 92b.lf.; tr. Suzuki [London: Routledge, 1932] pp. 65-67; discussed by R, p. 321).

24. "The relative" (saṁvṛti) refers to the conventional level of truth, as opposed to the "highest meaning" (paramārtha) alluded to by "right meaning" (samyag-artha)—the emptiness of all dharmas. Here the discussion continues, in terms of the six perfections, with the first: (dāna).

25. "Borrow from others" (paralābha) puns on "abuse others" (parābhava). The person indulging in alcohol tends, in his drunken state, to commit other misdeeds.

26. "All formations are impermanent" (sarva-saṁskārā anityāḥ). See E s.v. *saṁskāra; Dhammapada* v. 277. Saṁskāras—all worldly things—are "formed" by causes and conditions; arising, they must have an end—thus they are "impermanent." "Modes of impermanence": for discursive meditations on impermanence see for example VM 21.48: sees all formations as impermanent for the following reasons: because they are noncontinuous, temporary, limited by rise and fall . . . ." The *Laṅkāvatāra* discusses eight forms of impermanence (tr. pp. 176f.).

27. "Momentariness" (kṣaṇika) of objects is again the relative level of truth. All dharmas should be understood, in the higher sense, to have no arising at all. See *Laṅkāvatāra* P Ngu 165a.2f.:

As "empty, impermanent, momentary,"
The foolish conceive formations;
By the examples of river, lamp and seed,
They conceive the sense of "momentary."

Unformed and momentary,
Isolated, eliminated,
Dharmas are without birth:
Thus I explain the sense of "momentary."

See also *Bodhicaryāvatāra* 9.7-8.

28. This may be read: "Since by renouncing giving as the cause, one should obtain the loss of great enjoyment as the result . . . " "Great enjoyment" alludes to the *mahā-sāṁbhoga (-kāya)* of the Buddha, which represents the fruition of the merit of giving and other wholesome activities.

29. The three sufferings: pain or suffering per se, the change of previously pleasant feelings, and the general discomfort of formative existence (MHV 2228f, VM 16.35). The eight sufferings: birth, old age, sickness, death, dissociation from the pleasant, association with the unpleasant, not obtaining one's desires, (in short) the five grasping aggregates (or embodied existence).

Now he goes on to the second perfection, morality (śīla). For the bodhisattva, the salient feature of ethics is work for the welfare of others, rather than adherence to rules.

30. This defilement of "wrong view" springs from the vāsanā; see 46abc. The view of "self" is the primary wrong view. The four distortions (viparyāsa) are seeing permanence in the impermanent and pleasure, self and beauty in objects that lack these qualities (VM ch. 7, n. 25). On "distorted notions" in general—perceiving a nonexistent characteristic—see R pp. 377f.

31. Among the seven forms of pride, this is asmi-māna (MHV 1949). *Tīrthika* is a term for the brahmanical schools, "those who frequent the *tīrthas*," or sacred bathing places.

32. The Tibetan rendering ('dod pa ni 'dod pa ste) fails to catch the nuance of the original definition, whatever it is. The first *'dod pa* would stand for *'dod-chags* (rāga), as the other basic defilements are also mentioned; the second must translate *kāma*.

33. "Sufferings of change" (vipariṇāma-duḥkhatā): see n. 29 above.

34. Verse numbered 221b-222a of the "Pramāṇāsiddhi" chapter of Dharmakīrti, *Pramāṇavārttika* (ed. S. D. Shastri, Varanasi: Bauddha Bharati, 1968). See P Tanjur Ce 212b.5-6 for a different translation into Tibetan.

35. Māra is lord of the highest level of the realm of sense desires (see n. 4 above), the Akaniṣṭha heaven. He threatens those who attempt to escape his realm.

36. "Spread" (tīvra) is a term for the intensification of defilement (MHV 7264, v. 45a below).

37. Seven anuśaya are listed at VM 22.60, of which this is the first.

38. On the connection of the Lord of the Dead (Yama) with Māra in Buddhist mythology see Alex Wayman in the *Indo-Iranian Journal* v. 2, pp. 44-73, 112-131.

39. The sentence carries a pun of "night" (mtshan-mo) upon "mark" (mtshan) that is probably not to be found in the original Sanskrit.

40. The "waning face of the moon" (kṛṣṇa-pakṣa) is a season of danger and a term for Māra's legion (E s.v. *śukla*).

41. "Potentiality for renewed existence" (bhava-śakti). This is latent tendency (vāsanā) as function. The regretful thought is intolerable in that it bears the seed or potentiality, sown by the misdeed, for an unfortunate rebirth. "Renewed existence" is that link of the twelvefold chain of dependent origination that represents the future result of activity. Note that the text reads *sred-par* (tṛṣṇa), so "potentiality/capacity for craving," a previous link of the chain; the sense would be much the same.

Here we enter a discussion of patience (kṣānti), translated in its various functions as patience, forbearance, acceptance, tolerance, acquiesence, constancy, etc.

42. "Suffering of rebirth" (jāti-duḥkha): see n. 29 above.

43. The snake is named śvasa-viṣa, "poison-breath" E s.v.).

44. "Hatred" (pratigha) has previously been translated by "resentment" and "annoyance." This passage, comparing it to a concealed serpent, confirms the sense of the Tibetan: "inner anger/hatred" (khong khro ba).

45. "Three trainings" (śikṣā): ethics, meditation and wisdom.

46. "Baked" (paridāgha): a prakṛtic term for the hot season (E s.v.).

47. They still have no use for farming.

48. Compare the *Laṅkāvatāra* (tr. Suzuki): "Because of the influence of habit-energy (vāsanā) that has been accumulating variously by false reasoning (vikalpa) since beginningless time, what here goes under the name of Ālayavijñāna is accompanied by the seven Vijñānas which give birth to a state known as the abode of ignorance" (p. 190). And, "Mahāmati, when it is understood that the objective world is nothing but what is seen of the Mind itself, the habit-energy of false speculations and erroneous discriminations which have been going on since beginningless time is removed, and there is a revulsion (or turning-back) at the basis of discrimination—this is emancipation, Mahāmati, and not annihilation" (p. 202).

49. "Frequented road in that direction": de lta bu'i phyogs kyi rgyun lam.

50. The "three aspects of Dharma" are canonical texts (āgama), practice of the path (adhigama)—especially of the three trainings—and the highest level of truth (paramārtha). The middle term is generally translated "comprehension," but it refers to the process rather than to the end.

51. "Three vehicles": of śrāvaka, pratyekabuddha and bodhisattva (see n. 5 above).

52. Or "in other situations"; or "with regard to others." The author now turns from his inability to help others to his inability to accept help from them—specifically, from the Buddha.

53. Or, "sharing with them."

54. These two images are repeated at *Bodhicaryāvatāra* 6.36. For these and other images that illustrate the dependence of karmic formations upon ignorance, see VM 17.63.

55. Variant: "from one's own karma."

56. "Projection" (vikurvaṇa), as though by magic.

57. Or, "Patience has other blessed qualities."

58. Patience, with all virtue, has the karmic results of physical beauty, power and influence in this and successive lifetimes. See Lin Li-Kouang, *L'Aide Mémoire de la Vraie Loie* (Paris, 1946), pp. 246f.

59. Or, "adventitiously": see comm. to 33d below.

60. "Breaking moral discipline": duḥśīla.

61. The "conceit" of ordinary qualities: the "greater conceit" (mahāmāna) at greater qualities. The latter is not found as one of the seven types of pride (n. 22 above).

62. "Latent tendencies" (anuśaya) are defilement as potentiality; "ensnarement" (paryavasthāna) is defilement as manifest in thought and conduct.

63. "Memory" (smṛti) or "mindfulness."

64. The verse has "pretense" (g.yo, śāṭhya) and "delusion" (sgyu, māyā), whereas the commentary has "dishonesty" (g.yo-sgyu, śaṭha). The former two are counted among the upakleśas; they refer to dishonesty by pretension to qualities and dishonesty by concealment of shortcoming (Geshe Dhargyey).

65. "The lower range of Māra" would indicate the lower levels of the realm of sense desire: hellish, ghostly and animal rebirths.

In the practice of the fifth perfection, dhyāna, one may work at developing either calm or insight (= wisdom, prajñā). Here begins a set of verses contrasting the two approaches to meditation.

66. "The five sensual objects" (kāma-viṣaya): objects of the five senses.

67. "Natural detachment from dharmas that comes of wisdom" (dharma-prakṛti-viviktatva prajñayā): the understanding that all phenomena are isolated (empty of essence) by their very nature, "because they are empty of any basis for visualization." See Conze, *Materials for a Dictionary of the Prajñāpāramitā Literature* (Tokyo: Suzuki, 1967), s.v. viviktatva.

68. "Acceptance-rejection" (compare their usage in the comment to 43a below) refers to intellectual judgment. On excitedness versus laxity, see VM 4.45-73.

69. "Wisdom is defined as . . ." (sva-sāmānya-dharmalakṣaṇa-yathābhūta-vyavacāraṇā iti prajñā): the Tibetan translator prefers *spyod-pa* to the more usual *dpyod-pa* in rendering *vyavacāraṇa* so as to relate it to "coursing" (spyod-pa, caramāṇa).

70. "Placing a yoke" (yuganaddha): the VM, describing the results of concentration, says: "And lastly, when equanimity [calm] was thus intensified, the states called concentration and understanding produced there occurred coupled together (yuganaddha) without either one exceeding the other" (4.117).

71. The flame is wisdom; the windshield is concentration.

72. "Mental stability," or "stations of consciousness" (vijñāna/citta-sthiti). See *Bodhisattvabhūmi* P Zhi 123a and commentary Ri 237a-b; VM ch. 7, n. 13; *Abhidharmakośa* index s.v.

73. On the four stages of meditative trance see VM ch. 4.

74. "Creator" (kāraka): the gods have an extensive not a limited fruition of good karma; but karma, not God, is creator of the world.

75. "Yoga": a term for meditative practice subsequent to the yoking (yuganaddha) of calm and insight (*Sgra* p. 92; see also comment to 50b below).

76. The basic doctrines of the auditors. The five aggregates (skandha) are empty of "I" and "mine" (the aggregate of consciousness is the basis for the view of "I," the other four are the basis for the view of "mine"). One realizes this through the four Noble Truths.

77. "Adamantine concentration" (vajropama-samādhi): the

highest stage of meditation and peak of existence (bhavāgra), from which flows the mystic intuition that leads to liberation. See sGam-po-pa, *Jewel Ornament of Liberation,* tr. H. V. Guenther (Berkeley: Shambhala, 1971), pp. 251-252, 257f.

78. "Nirvāṇa 'without remainder'" (nirupadhiśeṣa-nirvāṇa): this is likened by the auditors to the extinction of a flame.

79. "Thought of awakening" (bodhicitta): the awakened mind, progress toward that goal and the initial intention of reaching it. In the translation of this text, the latter two are sometimes distinguished in Tibetan as *byang chub tu sems,* the former as *byang chub kyi sems.* See for example 44d below.

80. "Three sorts of suffering": see n. 29 above. "Four manners of birth": from womb, egg, warmth/moisture and miracle (as with the gods).

81. "Resolving . . . and setting forth": the two aspects of bodhicitta, initial aspiration and subsequent practice. See Har Dayal, *The Bodhisattva Doctrine* (repr. Delhi: Motilal, 1970), p. 62.

82. "Mystic intuition constituting the knowledge of all modes" (sarvākāra-jña-jñāna): According to the *Abhisamayālaṁkāra* (after R, p. 128), "knowledge in all modes" is "revealed by the progressive discovery (adhigama) of factors that occasion the obtainment of buddhahood." In this system, *jñāna* is a synonym for the perfection of *prajñā;* it is the result, *prajñā* is the process.

83. "Perceived and perceiver" (grāhya-grāhaka): the objective and subjective poles of conceptual consciousness. "Undiffused": niṣ-prapañca.

84. Twelve forms of differentiation are discussed in the *Laṅkāvatāra* (there translated "discrimination," p. 110f.), of which this is the last: of bondage and emancipation.

85. Arjuna: the great archer of the *(Mahā)bharata.* The particle *eva* has its usage in logic here.

86. This presents the Cittamātra theory of the *Laṅkāvatāra.* This quote again from the *Lavaṇa-nadī?*

87. Referring to mind as "support" (āśraya) and external objects as "supported" (āśritya) suggests the doctrine of store consciousness (ālaya-vijñāna).

88. Or, "method of the sūtras."

89. Variant: "Even continuing to cultivate, he is unable to dispel differentiation."

90. A variant of this dream analogy appears at *Bodhicaryāvatāra* 2.35. On dreams caused by differentiation see *Laṅkāvatāra,* translation p. 83, v. 149.

91. "Lord of all dharmas" (sarvadharma-adhipati): more specifically, "lord of unquestionable gnosis of all dharmas" (sarvadharma-niḥsaṁśaya-jñāna), MHV 362. See also Conze, *Materials* p. 417: "control, sovereignty, and overlordship over all dharmas" (sarvadharma-aiśvarya-adhipati-vaśavartitā).

92. "Misrepresentation" (abhūtaparikalpa): second of three svabhāvas of the Cittamātra school. The Tibetan (yang dag pa ma yin pa'i kun tu rtog pa) is not an exact translation of the Sanskrit, which means "the fabrication of what does not really exist." Vasubandhu defines the term as "differentiation of objective and subjective, the duality of perceiver and perceived (*Madhyāntavibhāga-bhāṣya* to 1.1; see R p. 323, with the subcomment by Sthiramati summarized afterward).

On "impressions" see n. 6 above.

93. "The four māras": kleśa-māra, skandha-māra, mṛtyu-māra and devaputra-māra. At n. 35 above, the last is in question; on the four, see ref. n. 38 above.

The gods are given five distinguishing qualities at *Abhidharmakośa* ch. 3, p. 137n. Added to these would be their long life?

94. "Responsible for their own actions" (karma-svaka): a common sentiment in Buddhist kāvya, see *Saundarananda* 16.17.

95. "Path of action" (īryā-patha): in this case, physical contact with disease.

96. Variant: "falling off."

97. Modern cures for leprosy must also be initiated at the beginning stages of the disease and continued for the duration of one's life.

98. Buddhists agree that saṁsāra has no beginning, for such would imply a primal cause. Whether it has an end, though, is tied to the question of whether all beings will attain nirvāṇa. If not all will do so, the Buddha's power of saving others must be limited; if all will, then his power likewise has an end. See R pp. 205-206, 223f., 231.

99. "Substance" (dravyatā) would seem to pun on sap (dravata).

100. "Mental gateway" (mano-dvāra): as distinguished from the gateways of body and speech.

101. "Philosopher's stone" (gser sgyur rtsi; rasāyana, dhātu-vāda): literally, "gold-transmuting potion." Śāntideva (*Bodhicaryāvatāra* 1.10) adopts this metaphor for bodhicitta, and Prajñākaramati, in his comment, refers to a potion called hāṭaka-prabhāsa that changes a thousand times its weight of iron into gold. In Śāntideva's image this human body will be transmuted, by awakening, into the (saṁbhoga-) kāya of a buddha. In Yogācāra terminology, it effects a transmutation ("conversion," parāvṛtti) of the mental storehouse (ālaya) from a state of defilement to that of purity (*Laṅkāvatāra,* tr., introd. pp. xvii f.; R s.v. *parāvṛtti* etc.).

102. "Generation of the intention" (cittotpāda): the initial resolve to attain awakening.

103. Variant: "tried."

104. "Mundane and supramundane qualities": awakening as the endeavor and as supreme wisdom.

105. "Inherently logical" (svabhāva-hetu): true by definition, by identity. By cittotpāda one joins the family (gotra) of the Buddha; this gotra becomes a natural cause of awakening, for it is full of good qualities by its very nature (see R, esp. pp. 89-90).

At this point of the *Praise* the author begins again from faith, this time conjoined with bodhicitta.

On *svabhāva-hetu* (opposed to *kārya-hetu*) see Th. Stcherbatsky, *Buddhist Logic* vol. 2 (repr. New York: Dover, 1962), pp. 70 n. 2, 122 n. 3, 127 n. 1, etc. (index s.v.); and Ernst Steinkellner, "On the Interpretation of the Svabhāvahetuḥ" in *WZKS* 1974, esp. pp. 123-124.

106. Variant: "If that relevance capable of eliminating the defilements does not exist, there ensues defeat by the defilements."

107. A series of allusions to the stages of spiritual progress that are being traversed. The "noble path of meditation instructions" (dhyānopadeśa) refers to the process of learning in the stages: hearing (śravaṇa) the topic, contemplation (cintā) of it and meditative development (bhāvanā) of it. By this process of learning one traverses five "paths" to awakening. In the commentary, "devotion" (adhimukti) alludes to the preparatory stage of the bodhisattva, including the paths of accumulation (sambhāra) and application (prayoga). Discerning indicates the third path, the darśana-mārga. The fourth and fifth, alluded to below, are "development" or "cultivation," and buddhahood.

The "stage of coursing in devotion" (adhimukticaryā-bhūmi) is defined thus (*Sgra* p. 44): "During one Incalculable Age the bodhisattva develops an inclination (adhimukti) toward the Dharmadhātu. Because he does not as yet see suchness (tathatā), he is 'coursing in devotion'" By "discerning the principle," the author has left this stage behind.

108. "Developing the path" refers to the fourth stage, the bhāvanā-mārga.

109. The three wisdoms are produced by the three stages of learning. See n. 107 above.

110. "Attitude" is *sems, citta.* "Predisposition is *bsam pa, āśaya;* not to be confused with *bsam pa* as rendering for *dhyāna,* "meditation," and for *cintā,* "contemplation" in this same passage.

111. "Subtle extensions" (phra rgyas rnams) is the Sarvāstivāda conception of "latent tendency," anuśaya. *Sgra* says (p. 116): "When applied to abhidharma texts, it [anuśaya] abides pervading the mental continuum of a living being until the noble gnosis has been attained, but it is hard to examine; it is subtle and, in conjunction with images, it causes the spread or extension of defilement. It is a term for an ocean bird, a shark that reaches at shadows flying by in the sky. In the Sautrāntika view, anuśaya is found latent as a mode of vāsanā [bag chags, 'impressions'], before the defilements have become manifest."

112. The eighteen "elements" (dhātu) that constitute a living being; also the elemental organism as manifest defilement. According to *Sgra*

(p. 117), *dhātu* is an older term for *gotra,* "class;" it refers to one's spiritual genus. See R p. 468.

113. "Signs . . . and proportions" (lakṣaṇa, anuvyañjana): listed MHV 235f., 268f. These are, strictly speaking, marks of the sambhoga-kāya. On "possession of the topknot" (uṣṇīṣa-siraskatā) see E s.v.

114. The Jambu is a river with golden sands that flows from the fruit of the Jambu tree on top of Mount Sumeru. See ref. at VM 1, n. 37; L. Hurvitz, *Scripture of the Lotus Blossom of the Fine Dharma* (New York: University Press, 1976), p. 252 n.

115. "Faculty of life" (jīvitendriya): one of twenty-two human faculties of the system of the *Abhidharmakośa* (ch. 2).

116. "He is the very reality of Dharma" (dharma-svabhāvāsti): besides cognizing the Buddha's body and voice, he knows his mind, the corpus of subtle Dharma, the absolute reality of things. The absolute is indemonstrable (anidarśana) because definition implies distinction (viśeṣa) and characteristic (lakṣaṇa); the Dharmabody is therefore beyond description (avācya, etc.; R pp. 381f.).

117. That is to say, the compound is a karmadhāraya.

118. The sun is a frequent metaphor for Dharma, which illumines the purities of dharmas (R p. 316). But as the next line will indicate, the Dharmabody is seen only by bodhisattvas whose faculties are at least partially purified. The auditors, independent buddhas and ordinary persons have at best the sphere of nirvāṇa, the nirvāṇa-dhātu as their object, not that of pure Dharma (R p. 378, and v. 36 above). The positive reality of the Dharmabody is a doctrine of the third and highest cycle of sūtra (R pp. 313-318, 381).

"'Sphere of Dharma' intuition" (dharmadhātu-jñāna) refers to the first of five jñānas associated with a buddha, called "purified sphere of Dharma" (dharmadhātu-pariśuddha). *Sgra* defines this jñāna thus (pp. 17.18):

Acting as the cause or element [dbyings, dhātu] for the birth and emergence of noble dharmas such as power and courage, we have "element of Dharma." The cloudlike obscurations (of adventitious defilement and the knowable) to suchness have been clarified or purged. On the model of "purified sphere of space," we have "purified sphere of Dharma."

Under the entry *dharma-kāya, Sgra* (pp. 19-20) calls Dharmabody "the purification of the sphere of Dharma, with mirrorlike intuition as its essential nature."

119. The first reference to bodhisattva "stages" (bhumi). On *buddha* as absolute reality see R pp. 347f.

120. The "high mind" (thugs mchog) is of course bodhicitta.

"Nondual mystic intuition" (advaya-jñāna) is nonconceptual understanding of the ultimate equality of all things. Dignāga defines Perfect Wisdom as "nondual intuition—the Tathāgata" (cited R p. 432).

121. "Wonderworking powers" (ṛddhi) are sometimes listed as a subset of "miracles" (prātihārya) and encompass multiple emanations and so forth. The other two types of miracle are mindreading (ādeśanā) and admonition (anuśāsana) "effecting the destruction of someone's vice." See MHV 231-234, E s.v. *prātihārya.*

122. The autumn moon appears bright and clear after the monsoon has cleared the air of dust.

Index

Sanskrit equivalents are reconstructions.

T